FISH ON
THE GRILL

FISH ON THE GRILL

BY THE EDITORS OF
TIME-LIFE BOOKS

TIME-LIFE BOOKS INC., ALEXANDRIA, VIRGINIA

Cover design: Tracey Smith
Cover photograph: Renée Comet
Food stylist: Lisa Cherkasky
Props courtesy of The Farrell Collection, Washington, D.C.
Book design: Karin Martin

Produced by Rebus, Inc.
New York, New York

First printing.

Printed in U.S.A.

Published simultaneously in Canada

TIME-LIFE is a trademark of Time Warner Inc. U.S.A.

Library of Congress Cataloging-in-Publication Data

Fish on the grill/by the editors of Time-Life Books.

p. cm.

ISBN 0-8094-6716-X

1. Cookery (Fish) 2. Cookery (Shellfish) 3. Barbecue cookery.

I. Time-Life Books.

TX747.F497 1994

641.6'92--dc20   93-46199
                        CIP

TABLE OF CONTENTS

A Guide To
Outdoor Cooking

Despite the obvious differences in size, shape, and design, all outdoor cooking equipment is based on two components: a firebox that holds the coals or other heat source and a rack or spit that holds the food to be grilled. As the five types of portable charcoal cookers described below demonstrate, these elements can be put together in a variety of ways.

The *brazier*, for example, is no more than a firebox and rack, and the fire is laid directly on the bottom of the firebox. In some models, the rack is supported on a central post that can be raised or lowered with a crank to adjust the temperature at which foods grill; in other models, the rack rests on notched brackets attached to the rim of the firebox, and the rack is adjusted by moving it from one set of notches to another. Legs (often with wheels) elevate the cooker to a convenient height. Some braziers also have a windscreen, or hood, that attaches to the firebox rim. Shaped like a half cylinder, the hood can be fitted with an electric or battery-powered rotisserie.

In a *hibachi*, by contrast, the fire is laid on a grate rather than on the bottom of the firebox. The addition of a grate permits air flow under the coals, which consequently burn hotter and more evenly. Vents near the bottom of the firebox can be opened or closed to regulate the air supply and thus the rate of burning. Hibachis usually have brackets for adjusting the height of the racks.

A *kettle grill* also contains a grate for the fire and has firebox vents to regulate the heat. Its rack, however, is not adjustable. In some models the vent closing device doubles as a sweeper to push ashes into an ash catcher below the firebox. But the principal feature of the kettle grill is its vented cover. Grilling food under a cover shortens its cooking time by as much as 25 percent and intensifies its smoky flavor.

A *rotisserie grill* has a grate, vents in the firebox, and a vented cover. The rack height can be adjusted by means of levers at the front of the grill. The rotisserie is supported by brackets that permit raising and lowering the spit rod. Some models include a cutting board that can be fixed to the edge of the firebox at either side.

Although smoking is a traditional method for preserving certain foods, modern *charcoal-water smokers* are only designed for cooking, not preserving. The smoker holds a pan for fuel and—above it—another pan for water and one or two for racks of food. Its tight-fitting cover traps smoke released by the green hardwood that is used to augment the charcoal fire; meanwhile the water pan provides steam to keep the food on the racks above it moist. In addition to serving as a smoker, the device may be used as a grill if the cover and water pan are removed and the charcoal pan placed directly under a rack.

Last, and of a completely different nature, are the *gas and electric grills*. In these, a layer of volcanic rock heats until it glows like a bed of coals. Although this heat source gives off no aroma of its own, and thus contributes no "grilled" flavor of to the food, these modern-day grills are admittedly convenient to use: They require all of about 10 minutes to preheat and the flame levels are easy to adjust. For some outdoor cooks, though, gas and electric grills take away half of the fun of a barbecue by removing nearly all of the challenge.

Except for the hibachi, which is often made of cast iron, the fireboxes and covers of grills and smokers are usually made of sheet steel. For durability and good heat retention, the steel should be 20-gauge or heavier; hot coals may burn a hole in light-gauge steel. The finish may be either porcelain enamel or heat-resistant paint. Of the two, porcelain enamel will stand up better to rust and heat.

Wire racks on an outdoor grill should be coated with nickel chrome, which resists flaking or pitting and thus keeps the wires easy to clean. Be sure that the rack is sturdy enough to prevent it from bending under the weight of a lot of food. Legs of portable cookers should be widely based for stability.

Before purchasing any grill or smoker, try out all of the vents, cranks, levers, hinges, wheels, and other moving parts to make sure that they operate properly. Look for handles that are easy to grasp. Wood and phenolic plastic handles absorb less heat than metal ones.

Maintaining Your Outdoor Cooker

Simple regular maintenance will extend the life of any cooker. One way of preserving the finish is to line the firebox with heavy-duty aluminum foil before building a fire, remembering to cut a hole in the foil where it overlies a vent. When the food is cooked and the fire is dead, the cooker should be left to cool; then the rack or rotisserie and grate can be removed and the ashes wrapped in the foil and discarded. If the firebox is not lined with foil, the cold ashes can be shoveled out or the grill inverted to dump them.

After each use, clean the rack with a stiff wire brush to remove the cooked-on grease and food. Wash the spit rod and holding forks of a rotisserie with soapy hot water and dry them well with a towel.

Before storing a grill or smoker for the winter, wash it thoroughly and dry each part. Then place it, if possible, in a dry, protected area such as a garage or basement. If it must be stored outdoors, use a tarpaulin or plastic cover to ward off rust.

About Fire

Successful cooking with coals depends on a good fire—hot enough to sustain a constant heat, but not so intense that it burns the food. And a good fire depends on the proper use of fuel.

For an outdoor grill, either lump charcoal or charcoal briquets will suffice. Lump charcoal, which is pure carbonized wood with no additives, is easy to light and burns fast. It produces a bed of usable embers in as little as 20 minutes, but may need to be replenished in another half-hour—which can require care and some dexterity if it entails removing a hot rack.

Charcoal briquets are basically composed of pulverized charcoal bound with cornstarch, although these ingredients are often augmented by mineral coal, sodium nitrate to aid ignition, and lime to retard the rate of burning. Denser than lumps, briquets burn longer but are slower to ignite: They may take 40 minutes or more to produce usable embers.

Whether you use lump charcoal or briquets, most grilling will require a bed about 2 inches deep and 1 to 2 inches larger than the area covered by the food. (For spit-roasting or grilling over a drip pan, you will need enough coals to form rows about 4 inches deep in front and in back of the pan.) In either case, start by piling the charcoal in a mound so that the fire will spread quickly and evenly.

An electric starter is a very useful addition to any cook's outdoor grilling accessories. Almost unfailingly, a starter will ignite the fire. Be careful to follow the instructions on the package; an overheated electric starter can burn out and melt. Other alternatives for starting the fire include petroleum-based liquids and jellies, but they may impart an undesirable taste to the food. Such products must be used with caution; once you get even the faintest glimmer of a fire under way, do not add any more starter. And never use gasoline or kerosene: Both are dangerously explosive.

After the fire is under way and the coals have burned long enough to acquire a coating of white ash, the coals should be rearranged for grilling or for spit-roasting. To judge whether coals have reached the proper temperature—a very important moment for successful, and succulent, outdoor cooking—hold the palm of your hand about 4 to 6 inches above the fire. Then count the seconds (one thousand one, one thousand two, etc.). If you must withdraw your hand after two seconds, the fire is hot and suitable for searing foods quickly. If you can tolerate the heat for four seconds, the fire is medium hot and suitable for grilling or roasting. If you can hold your palm over the coals for longer than that, the fire is not ready.

As to maintaining the heat of the fire, by opening all the vents on the grill you can increase the temperature of the fire; by closing them partially you will reduce it. Tapping the coals to remove their insulating cover of ash will also increase the heat, so will pushing them close together; spreading the coals apart will cool the fire down.

Neither charcoal lumps nor briquets are safe to use in any

enclosed space such as an indoor fireplace: Charcoal releases carbon monoxide in quantities that can be fatal. To grill or roast indoors in a fireplace, use wood logs as your fuel. The flames will force whatever carbon monoxide the wood generates up the chimney. The logs will burn down to produce embers suitable for grilling.

ABOUT SMOKE

Fish and shellfish are particularly appealing when grilled over natural materials—wood chips, herbs, seasonings, and so on—that yield fragrant smoke. Among the most popular aromatic woods are hardwoods and fruitwoods such as oak, alder, hickory, cherry, and apple. To make wood chips or chunks burn slowly and smokily, soak them before grilling in water (chips for half an hour, chunks for two hours), then place them on a wood or charcoal fire. (Should you be barbecuing over a gas grill, place the wood chips in a small foil baking pan and set it on the lava rocks or on on the bars above the gas jets. For electric grills, place the wood chips in the bottom of the grill, under the heating element. Start grilling as soon as the wood begins to smoke.)

Perhaps the best-known grilling wood is mesquite, a shrublike hardwood native to Mexico and the American Southwest that is sold as chips, chunks, or natural charcoal. The charcoal imparts a milder flavor than the wood but yields a hotter flame that cooks food quickly.

It follows that different woods complement different foods: Alder is traditionally chosen for salmon and trout. Fruity apple and cherry woods lend a smoky sweetness to mild-flavored shellfish. The compelling, assertive flavor of mesquite is best used for sturdy fish steaks, like shark or swordfish.

Grapevine cuttings will also create savory smoke, exuding a mild, winy aroma especially suited to fish and shellfish. First soak the vines in water, then place them on the fire for the last ten minutes of cooking time. Corncobs (dried for a few days after the kernels are removed) produce a fragrance similar to that of hickory. And pecans, almonds, or walnuts in their shells (soak the nuts briefly after partially cracking them) add their own distinct aromas to grilled seafood.

Herbs and other seasonings can also be used to scent the smoke. Soak fresh or dried herbs for half an hour before placing them on the coals: Try dill, rosemary, tarragon, or cilantro. Or, grill on fennel branches. For a lively tang, toss citrus rinds, or whole spices such as cloves or cinnamon sticks, onto the coals.

It has been said that where there is smoke, there is fire, and some fires can be made very flavorful, particularly when it comes to grilling fish and shellfish.

A Barbecuer's Batterie

A collection of certain tools designed specifically for barbecuing can not only enhance the experience of outdoor cooking, but help to keep it safe. Often the essential accoutrements come in a set that includes:

- A metal spatula, with a long wooden handle
- Metal tongs, with long wooden handles
- A basting brush, natural bristles preferred, with a long wooden handle
- A wire brush for scraping down the metal grilling rack

Very nice to have on hand as well are:

- An easy-to-wash long apron
- A squeeze bottle (for water) for dousing any flare-ups
- A set of bamboo skewers
- A set of metal skewers, preferably with decorative ends
- A hinged grilling basket
- A porcelan-coated metal grilling tray
- A collection of nonbreakable outdoor dinnerware

FISH & SHELLFISH

FISH AND SHELLFISH ON THE GRILL

The thought is as welcome as a breath of ocean air on a hot July day: Fish and shellfish contain more native goodness, ounce for ounce, than almost any other type of food. From the briny tang of a freshly shucked oyster to the majestic savor of salmon, they are as healthful as they are delicious. Fish provide one of the most concentrated sources of high-quality protein, they deliver an uncommonly rich supply of vitamins and minerals, and they are easily digested.

At the same time, most varieties recommend themselves to weight-conscious diners. A four-ounce portion of baked cod, for example, has fewer than 100 calories and only 1 gram of fat. Even their fattier cousins, such as king salmon and shad, have less than half the calories of a T-bone steak. Moreover, nearly all fish and shellfish are low in cholesterol. Even the folk wisdom that holds fish to be "brain food" may have some basis in fact: Studies have suggested that the fatty acids present in fish may be involved in the development of neural tissue.

More than 200 species of edible fish, not to mention a profusion of shellfish, thrive in North American waters. There is something to please every palate and accommodate every pocketbook. Flounder and sole have long been relished at the table, as have snapper and swordfish. But other, less well-known fish are available, too, and they offer exciting culinary opportunities. Fish and shellfish not only rank high nutritionally, they are among some of the simplest foods to prepare, particularly so when cooked on an outdoor grill.

SOME SURPRISING DISCOVERIES

It has long been known that fish and shellfish bestow a generous nutritional dividend, but until quite recently no one knew just how significant the health payoff could be. The long-held belief that fatty fish should be avoided due to its suspected relationship to heart disease had been overturned. In fact, quite the opposite is true: Fish fat has virtues all of its own. Scientists have determined (following studies of the eating habits of such fish-eating and notably heart-disease-free groups as Greenland Eskimos, middle-aged men in the Netherlands, and inhabitants of Japanese fishing villages) that fish contain certain polyunsaturated fats found in no other foods. Moreover, these substances have been demonstrated to have a profound effect on body chemistry: Fish oil contains certain types of polyunsaturated fatty acids—known as omega-3's—that appear to lower the levels of harmful triglycerides (fats) in the blood. In addition, fish oil behaves quite differently from polyunsaturated vegetable oils in staving off heart disease. The oils from such rich-fleshed swimmers as salmon and mackerel actually discourage the formation of blood clots that can block ailing arteries. Fish oil may also be beneficial in reducing the symptoms of such inflammatory diseases as psoriasis and arthritis.

And as if all of these health benefits were not enough to make seafood lovers smile, scientists have made some important discoveries about shellfish as well. Improved analytical techniques have revealed not only that most shellfish are low in cholesterol but that some, notably the shelled mollusks, contain sterols picked up from their vegetarian diet that actually appear to reduce the amount of dietary cholesterol absorbed by the body. And only a very small number of shellfish—squid, octopus, shrimp, razor clams, blue crab, and black abalone—have more than 100 milligrams of cholesterol per 3½-ounce portion, rendering them less recommendable to people on low-cholesterol diets.

Further enhancing the reputation of fish and shellfish for being healthful food are their stores of vitamins and minerals. The B vitamins, which the body needs to make proper use of protein and other nutrients, are particularly abundant in tuna, sardines, herring, and various shellfish. Healthy blood requires iron and copper, and most shellfish provide both; finned fish with dark meat, such as mackerel, are also good iron sources. A generous dose of phosphorus, essential for strong bones, comes with every fish course. All salt water varieties provide iodine, and most types provide potassium, fluoride, manganese, and magnesium as well. Oysters are exceptionally high in zinc, which helps fight infection, promotes healthy skin, and is used to build more than 100 vital enzymes important in the body's metabolic reactions (metabolism).

COMPARING FISH

THE FAT CONTENT OF FISH VARIES FROM SPECIES TO SPECIES, EVEN WITHIN A SPECIES, DEPENDING ON SEASON AND DIET. IT IS SIMPLEST TO THINK OF FISH, BOTH FROM A HEALTH STANDPOINT AND A COOKING STANDPOINT, AS "FATTY" OR "LEAN."

• FATTY FISH (WITH MORE THAN 5 GRAMS OF FAT IN A 3½ OUNCE SERVING) INCLUDE SALMONS, MACKERELS, ANCHOVIES, HERRINGS, SARDINES, AND BLUEFIN TUNAS.

• LEAN FISH (THOSE WITH LESS THAN 5 GRAMS OF FAT PER 3½ OUNCE SERVING) INCLUDE SNAPPERS, SOLES, CODS, FLOUNDERS, HADDOCKS, YELLOWFIN TUNAS, AND SEA BASSES AS WELL AS LOBSTERS, SHRIMPS, AND SCALLOPS.

TO SOME EXTENT, THE AMOUNT OF FAT IN A FISH OR SHELLFISH DETERMINES THE BEST COOKING METHOD FOR IT: FATTIER FISH ARE LESS LIKELY TO BECOME DRY WHEN COOKED BY DIRECT HIGH HEAT, AS IN GRILLING.

ADVICE FOR ANGLERS

Fish and shellfish rank among the most perishable of foods. The high moisture content of fish, in particular, offers bacteria an attractive environment in which to grow. In addition, oils present—particularly in the fattier types—begin to oxidize when they are exposed to air. Thus if you are a fisherman, or gather your own shellfish, special care must be paid to maintaining their freshness.

Knowledgeable anglers make it a practice to kill and gut each fish as soon as it is taken from the hook. Bacteria lodged in the digestive organs are the first cause of decomposition. To gut the fish, make a cut from the anal fin toward the head and draw out the viscera. Stow the cleaned fish in a cooler filled with crushed ice, or with ferns or seaweed in a creel or other container. Back in the kitchen, the fish can be scaled or skinned, or cut into fillets. If not cooked immediately, it can be rinsed, patted dry, wrapped tightly in plastic, and stored for three to five days in the coolest part of the refrigerator, with some enthusiasts suggesting you put it on a bed of crushed ice. Remember that the fish, even when stored correctly, will lose freshness with each passing day.

Many people like to gather their own shellfish, raking up clams from the shore, setting a crab line, or prying a feast of mussels from rocks or pilings. Provided that the source is an unpolluted body of water, the rewards at the table cannot be paralleled. Check with the local fish and game commission or the department of public health to be sure the area is safe. Whatever is collected can be preserved for a day or two in the refrigerator in open containers covered with a damp cloth, but do not keep it any longer.

WHAT TO LOOK FOR AT THE MARKET

Most of us do our fishing at the market, but a few simple guidelines will help bring home the freshest catch available. The first priority is to find a reliable supplier—and the signs of the really good fish market are immediately evident. Every surface should be scrupulously clean, and a sweet, briny fragrance should fill the air. The fish will be laid, often arranged artistically, on crushed ice in refrigerated display cases. The ice should be sparkly and clean, as should any containers. Good vendors will cut only as many fillets and steaks as they know they can sell that day, for fish keeps best when left whole. There may be a tank of live lobsters in seawater—notice if the lobsters are moving—or a bin of iced crabs still twitching their claws.

Not too long ago, the choice of what to buy in the fish market was based upon what was freshest and, frequently, what was in season, for it was the cheapest. Now, with nationwide distribution of commercial fish so efficient, with shipments being sent out from processing centers by refrigerated truck or airplane on a daily basis, the mere selection of what to buy can be staggering. Furthermore, thanks to aquaculture—fish farming—such seasonal species as rainbow trout, catfish, and salmon are often available, not only on a daily basis, but year round.

JUDGING FRESHNESS

• If appropriate or possible, buy a whole drawn or dressed fish. A drawn fish is one that is scaled, with the viscera and gills removed. A dressed fish ia a drawn fish with the head, tail, and fins removed.

• The advantage to buying a whole fish is that it will have been handled less and will have lost fewer of its juices.

• When a whole fish is truly fresh, its eyes will be clear, bright, and slightly protruding, and the pupils will be shiny. The gills should be pinkish or bright red; brown gills signal a less-than-fresh specimen. The skin should be firm and bright, with the scales adhering to it tightly. The flesh of most fish should feel firm and elastic to the touch.

• It is the smell of the fish, though, that to many is the telltale sign: It should be fresh, with a subtle clean fragrance suggestive to some of cucumber, to others of the sea itself. A fishy odor is a sure sign of deterioration. Be aware that members of the shark and skate families give off a slight ammonia scent, but that is as it should be and will disappear.

• The task of identifying truly fresh fish is more difficult when it comes to steaks or fillets, but here, too, appearances count. Each piece should be firm and its cut surfaces should be moist, not dried out, with no sliminess and no browning or yellowing at the edges. Nor should there be any smell of fishiness. If the fish is prepackaged there should be little air space between the fish and wrapping, and little or no liquid in the package. Do not purchase any fish with milky-colored fluid in the bottom of the packing tray.

• If you are electing to buy frozen fish, bear in mind that any intermediate thawing and refreezing between the processing center and the store counter (or between the home freezer and table, for that matter) will take an unfortunate toll. Only buy packages that are frozen solid, without interior air pockets. Reject any that have torn wrappings or exterior coatings of frost. Discoloration of the fish is a sure sign of freezer burn, which occurs when moisture is lost through faulty packaging and which destroys flavor.

HOW MUCH SEAFOOD TO BUY

The amount of seafood to buy, whether frozen or fresh, depends on how it will be cooked, and of course on how much is to be eaten. General guidelines suggest that a standard portion of fish or shellfish runs about 4 to 6 ounces of cooked meat, not counting bones or shells.

• With a whole, but drawn fish, you should allow as much as 12 ounces for each diner.

• For a fish that has already been dressed, about 8 ounces per person will be ample.

• Half a dozen clams or oysters make the customary half-shell first course.

• When buying shrimp, remember that about half their weight consists of heads and shells.

ENSURING FLAVOR AND NUTRITION

Seafood tastes best when it is promptly used. If fish cannot be cooked on the day of its purchase, it should be rinsed in cold water, dried with paper towels, tightly wrapped in plastic wrap, and stored for up to two days in the coolest part of the refrigerator.

Longer intervals of storage require that the fish be frozen. Whether it is purchased at the store or proudly borne home from a morning's fishing expedition, the method is the same. The gutted fish should be scaled, if necessary; it can then be cut into fillets, steaks or chunks, or kept whole, as desired. After rinsing the fish under cold running water, pat it dry with paper towels and wrap it in aluminum foil or moistureproof plastic, with as much air pressed out as possible; air is the archvillain of freezer burn. The packets should be placed in the freezer to promote rapid chilling. If the freezer temperature is held down to a frigid 0° F, fatty fish can be stored for up to three months, and leaner varieties for six months. But for the best flavor, all frozen fish should be used within one or two months.

And when it comes to shellfish, do not even attempt to freeze them; some, like shrimp, may have already been frozen because of their perishability. Refreezing shellfish serves only to rob it of more flavor and texture.

In thawing fish, defrost each packet in the refrigerator, well in advance of the time the fish is to be cooked; allow 24 hours for each pound. Do not thaw fish at room temperature; bacteria will quickly start to grow. Once the fish is defrosted, wash it again gently and dry it once more to get rid of any bacteria that might be present on the surface.

PREPARING FISH AND SHELLFISH FOR GRILLING

As the nineteenth-century French gastronome Brillat-Savarin wrote in The Physiology of Taste, "fish in the hands of a skilled cook can become an inexhaustable source of gustatory pleasures." The same can be said of shellfish. Whether served hot or cold, fish and shellfish are indispensable to creative cooks. And when grilled over open flames, they can be exquisite.

Fish and shellfish are two very different forms of aquatic life. A fish is a vertebrate, an animal with a backbone that breathes with gills and propels itself by means of fins. The term *shellfish* applies to certain edible mollusks and crustaceans. All shellfish are invertebrates, animals that lack a backbone and most often have some kind of shell. Crustaceans, which have jointed feet and a hard external skeleton, include lobsters, shrimps, prawns, crabs, and crayfishes. Mollusks that are enclosed in a hard shell include clams, mussels, oysters, and scallops. Mollusks that have an internal shell or no shell at all include octopuses, squids, and cuttlefishes.

CLEANING FISH

Although most supermarkets and retail fish stores sell fresh fish already drawn or dressed, good cooks should know how to prepare their own fresh fish.

• With a few exceptions, such as flounder and trout, fish require scaling, which is done with a knife or special implement. First, rinse the fish in cold water, then lay the wet fish on a flat surface. Grasp the tail with one hand and hold a sharp knife vertically (perpendicular to the fish) in the other. Scrape off the scales with the blunt side of the blade from tail end forward, in short, firm strokes.

• To gut a round fish, use a sharp knife to slit open the stomach from the head to the vent (located about one third the length of the fish anterior to the tail), then pull out the viscera. Remove the blood line, at the base of the backbone, and clean the cavity to remove the membrane by rubbing with a little coarse salt.

• To gut a flat fish, make a small cut in the belly behind the gills and pull out the viscera.

• If you plan to grill (or cook in another manner) any fish whole, you must remove the tough, bitter gills: Reach through the gill opening and pull out the gills. If you wish to remove the head, cut straight down behind the gills. Cut away the fins for easier cooking and eating and for a more attractive presentation. Rinse the cleaned fish well inside and out, under cold running water, carefully removing any remaining scales. Pat it dry with paper towels.

FILLETING FISH

Whole fish and steaks are almost always cooked with their skin intact, but for fillets, you will usually remove both skin and bones.

• To fillet a round fish, place the cleaned fish, with or without the head, on a flat surface, with the head pointing away from you. With a long sharp flexible-blade knife, slice through the flesh from just behind the head to the tail to expose the backbone. Next, just behind the gill, slice straight down to the backbone. Grasping the head with one hand and holding the knife horizontally, insert the knife at the head and slice the flesh away from the backbone in short strokes. Then, lift off the whole side of the fish in one piece. Turn the fish over and repeat this process on the other side. Run your fingertips along the inside of the fillet to check for any remaining bones: Remove the larger ones with your fingers, the smaller ones with tweezers.

• To skin the fillets, lay the fillet, skin-side down, on a flat surface. Insert the knife blade between the skin and the flesh at the tail end, and carefully slice the skin off of the flesh. Repeat the process with the other fillet.

• Flat fish are usually skinned *before* being filleted. To skin, make a shallow cut in the skin at the tail. Then, hold the tail firmly in one hand and, grasping the skin tightly with the other, peel it off of the fish. Repeat the process on the other side.

• To fillet a flat fish, with or without the head, lay the fish on a flat surface. Insert the knife tip at the head end and cut along the backbone to the tail. Slip the blade under the flesh, and gently cut the flesh away from the bones, working from head to tail, to remove the fillet in one piece. Cut away the second fillet in the same way, and then turn the fish over and repeat the process on the other side. You will have four fillets.

HANDLING SHELLFISH

You may wish to purge bivalves (clams, mussels, and oysters). To do this, place the live bivalves, in their shells, in a gallon of cold water with one teaspoon of sea salt and one cup of cornmeal, and let sit for at least 3 hours.

Clams: With a stiff brush, scrub the clams under cold running water to remove any surface mud. To shuck, hold the clam over a bowl to catch the liquor and insert the blade of a clam knife or a wide, rounded-end blade between the shells opposite the hinge. Twist

the blade to force the shell halves apart, then slide the cutting edge of
the blade along the inside to cut apart the muscles holding the shells
together.

Mussels: With a stiff brush, scrub the mussels under cold running
water to remove any surface mud. Remove the beard and pull off any
strands that stick out of the shell. Using a scrubbing brush or knife,
scrape off any surface encrustations.

Oysters: With a stiff brush, scrub the oysters under cold running
water. To shuck, hold the oyster, with the flatter shell upmost, over a
bowl to catch the liquor and insert the tip of an oyster knife into the
hinge. Twist the knife to open the shells, then slide the knife along
the inside of the upper shell to cut the muscle. Discard the upper
shell. To cut the oyster loose from the bottom shell, slice the knife
blade under the oyster.

Shrimp: These are usually sold without the head, but if they are
whole, twist off the head. To peel and devein, starting at the head
end, slip your thumb under the shell between the swimmerets. Lift off

IS IT DONE YET?

THE CANADIAN DEPARTMENT OF FISHERIES HAS DEVISED A SIMPLE,
FOOLPROOF GUIDE FOR CALCULATING THE COOKING TIME FOR FISH:
MEASURE THE FISH (WHOLE, FILLET, OR STEAK) AT ITS THICKEST PART.
FOR FRESH FISH, COOK IT 10 MINUTES FOR EVERY INCH OF THICKNESS;
FOR FROZEN, 20 MINUTES. THIS APPLIES TO ANY COOKING TECHNIQUE
FOR FISH BUT NOT FOR SHELLFISH. HOWEVER, WHEN GRILLING, CHECK
FOR DONENESS FREQUENTLY, PARTICULARLY WHEN COOKING THIN
FILLETS. INSERT THE TIP OF A SHARP KNIFE INTO THE FISH: THE FISH IS
JUST COOKED WHEN THE FLESH BARELY FLAKES, IS OPAQUE, AND DOES
NOT CLING TO THE BONE. THE COLOR OF THE OUTSIDE OF THE FISH IS
ALSO A VERY GOOD INDICATOR OF DONENESS AND KNOWING HOW
GOLDEN OR DEEPLY BROWNED THE OUTSIDE OF A GRILLED PIECE OF
FISH SHOULD BE COMES WITH EXPERIENCE.

two or three shell segments at once and, holding the tail, pull the shrimp out of the shell. If desired, pull off the tail shell, or leave it on for a decorative appearance. With a sharp paring knife, slit down the back and lift out the black vein.

Lobsters: For fresh lobsters, rinse briefly under cold running water prior to cooking.

Squid: Hold the head with one hand, the body with the other, and firmly pull the head away from the body. Cut off the tentacles and discard the remainder of the head. Pull the transparent quill-like piece out of the body sac and discard it. Wash the squid thoroughly inside and out, and peel the skin away from the body and fins. Slice the body into rings, if desired.

GRILLED COD WITH TOMATO AND BELL PEPPER RELISH

4 MEDIUM PLUM TOMATOES (ABOUT ¾ POUND TOTAL) OR 1 CAN (14 OUNCES) WHOLE TOMATOES, DRAINED

1 SMALL RED BELL PEPPER, HALVED, SEEDED, AND DERIBBED

3 SCALLIONS

¼ CUP FRESH BASIL LEAVES OR 1½ TEASPOONS DRIED

2 TABLESPOONS OLIVE OR OTHER VEGETABLE OIL

2 TABLESPOONS RED WINE VINEGAR OR CIDER VINEGAR

½ TEASPOON FRESHLY GROUND BLACK PEPPER

¼ TEASPOON SALT

4 COD OR HALIBUT STEAKS, EACH CUT ¾ INCH THICK (ABOUT 1 POUND TOTAL)

Preheat the grill. Spray the grill with nonstick cooking spray.

Coarsely chop the tomatoes and place in a bowl. In a food processor, coarsely chop the bell pepper, scallions, and basil. Transfer the vegetable mixture to the bowl with the tomatoes and stir in the oil, vinegar, black pepper, and salt until well combined. Strain the excess liquid from the tomato and bell pepper relish into a small bowl. Set the relish aside.

Place the cod steaks on the grill and brush them with some of the relish liquid. Grill the steaks 4 to 5 inches from the heat for 4 minutes, turn them, and brush with some more of the liquid. Grill the steaks until they are lightly colored, and the flesh just flakes when tested with a fork, about 4 minutes more. Transfer the fish steaks to a heated platter and top each of them with some of the tomato and bell pepper relish.

MENU

SKEWERED CANTALOUPE WRAPPED WITH PROSCIUTTO

GRILLED COD WITH TOMATO AND BELL PEPPER RELISH

HERBED NEW POTATOES, CARROTS, AND SCALLIONS (PAGE 97)

FRENCH BREAD GRILLED WITH GARLIC BUTTER

BROWNIES WITH HOT FUDGE SAUCE

ESPRESSO

GRILLED SWORDFISH WITH ANCHO CHILI SAUCE

SIX 5-OUNCE SWORDFISH STEAKS, CUT ½ TO ¾ INCH THICK

2 TABLESPOONS FRESH THYME LEAVES OR 2 TEASPOONS DRIED

3 CLOVES GARLIC, FINELY CHOPPED

JUICE OF 2 LEMONS

4 DRIED ANCHO CHILI PEPPERS, STEMMED AND SEEDED

1 QUART BOILING WATER

1 OUNCE (3 OR 4) OIL-PACKED SUN-DRIED TOMATOES

¾ CUP BOTTLED CLAM JUICE

½ CUP TAWNY PORT

2 TEASPOONS SAFFLOWER OIL

Preheat the grill. Spray the grill with nonstick cooking spray.

Rinse the swordfish steaks under cold running water and pat them dry with paper towels. In a shallow dish large enough to hold the steaks in one layer, combine the thyme, two-thirds of the garlic, and the lemon juice. Add the steaks and let them marinate, covered, in the refrigerator, turning them once or twice, for 1 hour.

In a heatproof bowl, cover the chilies with the boiling water and let them soak for 20 minutes.

Drain the chilies, discarding the water, and transfer them to a blender or food processor. Add the tomatoes and clam juice and purée the mixture.

In a nonreactive saucepan, bring the port to a boil over medium-high heat and cook it until it is reduced by half, 3 to 4 minutes. Stir in the chili-tomato purée and the remaining garlic. Reduce the heat to medium and cook the sauce, stirring occasionally, for 5 minutes. Strain the sauce through a fine sieve to cover the bottom of a heated platter.

Remove the swordfish steaks from the marinade and brush them with the oil. Grill the steaks 4 to 5 inches from the heat for 2 or 3 minutes per side, until the flesh is barely opaque when tested with the tip of a sharp knife. Arrange the steaks on the ancho chili sauce and serve immediately.

GRILLED MONKFISH SKEWERS WITH CILANTRO-LIME BUTTER

1 STICK (½ CUP) UNSALTED BUTTER, CUT INTO PIECES

2 SMALL CLOVES GARLIC, MINCED

2 TABLESPOONS FRESH LIME JUICE

½ TEASPOON SALT

1 SMALL BUNCH OF CILANTRO, RINSED, DRIED, AND MINCED

3 LIMES, QUARTERED LENGTHWISE

2 POUNDS MONKFISH CUT INTO 2-INCH CHUNKS (ABOUT 24 PIECES)

GRATED ZEST OF 1 SMALL LIME

Preheat the grill.

In a small saucepan, melt the butter over medium heat until the foam disappears. Add the garlic, lime juice, and salt and cook, stirring occasionally with a wooden spoon, for 1 to 2 minutes, or until heated through. Remove the pan from the heat and stir in 2 tablespoons of the minced cilantro.

On each of four 12-inch metal skewers, thread 1 lime wedge followed by 3 chunks of monkfish, another lime wedge, 3 more chunks of monkfish, and finish with a lime wedge. Using a pastry brush, coat each of the skewers generously with some of the cilantro-lime butter.

Grill the skewers 4 inches from the heat, turning them, for 8 to 10 minutes, or until the fish is golden brown and the flesh flakes easily when tested with the tip of a sharp knife.

Transfer the skewers to a heated platter, and drizzle them with the remaining butter. Combine the grated lime zest with an equal amount of the remaining minced cilantro and sprinkle it lightly over the hot skewers. Serve at once.

1 SMALL ONION, CUT INTO ¼-INCH
SLICES AND SEPARATED INTO RINGS

¼ CUP FRESH LEMON JUICE

4 TEASPOONS OLIVE OIL

½ TEASPOON SALT

½ TEASPOON FRESHLY GROUND
BLACK PEPPER

1½ POUNDS SWORDFISH STEAKS,
CUT 1 INCH THICK, SKINNED
AND CUT INTO 1-INCH CUBES

20 LARGE BAY LEAVES

2 CUPS BOILING WATER

BAY-SCENTED GRILLED SKEWERED SWORDFISH

In a deep bowl, combine the onion, 2 tablespoons of the lemon juice, 2 teaspoons of the oil, the salt, and pepper. Add the swordfish cubes, turning them to coat well. Let the fish marinate, covered, at room temperature for 2 hours or in the refrigerator for 4 hours, turning it occasionally.

In a heatproof bowl, cover the bay leaves with the boiling water and let them soak for 1 hour to prevent them from burning when grilled.

Preheat the grill. Spray the grill with nonstick cooking spray.

Drain the bay leaves and remove the swordfish cubes from the marinade. Thread the fish and bay leaves, alternating them, on four 10-inch metal skewers, pressing the pieces firmly together.

Combine the remaining 2 tablespoons lemon juice and 2 teaspoons oil and brush the lemon oil evenly over the fish.

Grill the skewers 4 to 5 inches from the heat, turning them every minute or so, until the fish is lightly colored and evenly cooked through, 6 to 7 minutes. Transfer the skewers to a heated serving platter and serve immediately. Discard the bay leaves.

MENU

BAY-SCENTED GRILLED
SKEWERED SWORDFISH

LEMON RICE PILAF

RATATOUILLE

BLUEBERRY TARTLETS

SERVES 4

GRILLED BLUEFISH WITH APPLE-ONION CREAM SAUCE

1 MEDIUM ONION

1 LARGE GRANNY SMITH APPLE,
UNPEELED IF DESIRED

2 TABLESPOONS UNSALTED BUTTER

¼ CUP FRESH LEMON JUICE

2 TABLESPOONS OLIVE OR OTHER
VEGETABLE OIL

2 TABLESPOONS DIJON MUSTARD

2 TEASPOONS GRATED LEMON ZEST

2 TEASPOONS CHOPPED FRESH DILL

¼ TEASPOON SUGAR

¼ TEASPOON FRESHLY GROUND
BLACK PEPPER

4 BLUEFISH FILLETS (ABOUT
1½ POUNDS TOTAL)

¼ CUP CHICKEN BROTH

2 TABLESPOONS SOUR CREAM

Preheat the grill. Spray a grilling basket with nonstick cooking spray.

Cut the onion and apple into thin wedges. In a medium skillet, warm the butter over medium-high heat until melted. Add the onion and cook until the onion begins to brown, about 5 minutes. Add the apple and sauté it until it begins to soften, about 3 minutes.

In a small bowl, combine the lemon juice, oil, mustard, lemon zest, dill, sugar, and pepper.

Arrange the bluefish fillets in the grilling basket and brush them with 2 tablespoons of the lemon-mustard mixture. Close the basket. Grill the fillets 4 to 5 inches from the heat for 4 to 5 minutes. Turn, brush them with a little more of the lemon-mustard mixture, and grill them for 4 minutes more, or until the flesh just flakes when tested with a fork.

Meanwhile, add the remaining lemon-mustard oil and the chicken broth to the skillet. Bring the mixture to a boil over medium-high heat and cook, uncovered, for about 3 minutes, until reduced slightly. Remove the pan from the heat and stir in the sour cream. Keep the sauce warm.

Transfer the bluefish fillets to a heated platter and top each with some of the warm apple-onion cream sauce.

GRILLED BLUEFISH WITH APPLE-ONION CREAM SAUCE

GRILLED FLOUNDER WITH LEMON CREAM

SERVES 4

2 TABLESPOONS UNSALTED BUTTER,
MELTED

¼ CUP FRESH LEMON JUICE

1 TABLESPOON GRATED LEMON ZEST

2 TEASPOONS CHOPPED FRESH TARRAGON
OR 1 TEASPOON DRIED

½ TEASPOON SALT

½ TEASPOON GROUND WHITE PEPPER

4 SMALL FLOUNDER FILLETS (ABOUT
1¼ POUNDS TOTAL) OR OTHER
FIRM-FLESHED WHITE FISH,
SUCH AS SOLE OR SNAPPER

1 TEASPOON DIJON MUSTARD

½ TEASPOON DRY MUSTARD

½ CUP HEAVY CREAM

GRILLED FLOUNDER WITH LEMON CREAM

Preheat the grill. Spray a grilling basket with nonstick cooking spray.

In a small bowl, combine the melted butter, 2 tablespoons of the lemon juice, 1 teaspoon of the lemon zest, 1 teaspoon of the tarragon, the salt, and pepper.

Place the flounder fillets on the grilling basket and brush them with some of the lemon-butter mixture. Grill the fillets 4 to 5 inches from the heat for about 7 minutes, turning them once, or until the fish is cooked through and the flesh just flakes when tested with a fork. The fillets will be lightly golden in color.

Meanwhile, in a bowl, combine the remaining 2 tablespoons lemon juice, 2 teaspoons lemon zest, 1 teaspoon tarragon, the Dijon mustard, and dry mustard. Gradually beat in the cream in a thin stream. Continue beating until the cream forms soft peaks.

Transfer the flounder fillets to a heated platter and top each of them with a dollop of the lemon cream. Serve at once.

MENU

**GRILLED FLOUNDER WITH
LEMON CREAM**

**DILLED CARROTS
AND SUMMER SQUASH**

**MIXED GREENS AND
SLICED TOMATOES**

PEAR TART

4 QUARTER-SIZE SLICES FRESH GINGER,
EACH ¼ INCH THICK, UNPEELED

2 CLOVES GARLIC

¼ CUP REDUCED-SODIUM SOY SAUCE

3 TABLESPOONS FRESH LIME JUICE

2 TABLESPOONS VEGETABLE OIL

1 TABLESPOON HONEY

1 TEASPOON GRATED LIME ZEST

¼ TEASPOON FRESHLY GROUND
BLACK PEPPER

¼ TEASPOON RED PEPPER FLAKES

1¼ POUNDS TUNA STEAKS

4 CUPS (ABOUT 6 OUNCES) SHREDDED
NAPPA OR CHINESE CABBAGE

4 CUPS (ABOUT ½ HEAD) SHREDDED
RED LEAF LETTUCE

2 LARGE CARROTS, PEELED AND CUT INTO
JULIENNE STRIPS

2 CUPS (ABOUT ¼ POUND) BEAN
SPROUTS, RINSED AND PATTED DRY

2 TABLESPOONS SESAME SEEDS,
TOASTED IF DESIRED

ORIENTAL WARM GRILLED TUNA SALAD

Preheat the grill. Spray the grill with nonstick cooking spray.

In a food processor, finely chop the ginger and garlic. Add the soy sauce, lime juice, oil, honey, lime zest, black pepper, and red pepper flakes and process to blend. Set aside half of the mixture to use as a salad dressing.

Brush the tuna steaks generously with some of the remaining ginger-garlic baste. Grill them 4 inches from the heat for 5 minutes. Turn the fillets and brush with any remaining baste. Grill until the flesh is lightly colored and just flakes when tested with a fork, about 5 minutes.

Divide the cabbage, lettuce, carrots, and bean sprouts evenly among 4 dinner plates. Cut the grilled tuna into ¾-inch chunks and place them on the salads. Pour the reserved salad dressing over all, then sprinkle with the sesame seeds. Serve while the tuna is still warm.

MENU

ORIENTAL WARM GRILLED
TUNA SALAD

GRILLED VEGETABLE KEBABS
(PAGE 89)

TOMATOES AND CUCUMBERS IN
HERBED VINAIGRETTE

GINGERED FRESH FRUIT
IN A WATERMELON BOAT (PAGE 121)

LEMON SQUARES

1 TABLESPOON VEGETABLE OIL

1 UNDERRIPE PAPAYA, PEELED, SEEDED,
AND CUT INTO 1-INCH PIECES

1 SMALL ONION, COARSELY CHOPPED

¼ TEASPOON SALT

½ CUP BOTTLED CLAM JUICE

⅓ CUP FRESH LIME JUICE

¼ CUP HEAVY CREAM

¾ TEASPOON RED PEPPER FLAKES

FOUR 6-OUNCE HALIBUT STEAKS

4 SCALLIONS, TRIMMED

GRILLED HALIBUT STEAKS WITH PAPAYA SAUCE

Preheat the grill.

In a 10- to 12-inch nonreactive skillet, heat the oil over medium heat, add the papaya, onion, and ⅛ teaspoon of the salt, and cook the mixture, stirring frequently, for 7 minutes. Pour in the clam juice and all but 1 tablespoon of the lime juice. Bring the liquid to a boil, reduce the heat to low, and simmer the mixture for about 10 minutes.

Transfer the papaya mixture to a food processor or blender and purée it until smooth, stopping once to scrape down the sides of the bowl.

In a heavy nonreactive 2- to 3-quart saucepan, combine the heavy cream and red pepper flakes over medium heat and simmer the mixture for 3 minutes, whisking often. Whisk the papaya purée into the hot cream, a spoonful at a time. Keep the sauce warm over low heat.

Sprinkle the halibut steaks with the remaining ⅛ teaspoon salt and the remaining 1 tablespoon lime juice. Grill the steaks 4 to 5 inches from the heat for 4 minutes. Turn the steaks and grill them until the flesh is firm to the touch, about 3 minutes.

While the halibut cooks, grill the scallions, turning them, until they are lightly charred all over and heated through.

Transfer the halibut steaks to a heated platter, and spoon the papaya sauce around them. Chop the grilled scallions coarsely and scatter them decoratively over the fish and sauce. Serve immediately.

SWORDFISH GRILLED WITH LEMON, TOMATO, AND BASIL SAUCE

3 TABLESPOONS DIJON MUSTARD

2 TABLESPOONS FRESH LEMON JUICE

2 TABLESPOONS OLIVE OR OTHER VEGETABLE OIL

2 TABLESPOONS FRESHLY GRATED PARMESAN CHEESE

1 TEASPOON CHOPPED FRESH BASIL LEAVES, PLUS ADDITIONAL CHOPPED LEAVES, FOR GARNISH

¼ TEASPOON SALT

¼ TEASPOON FRESHLY GROUND BLACK PEPPER

4 SWORDFISH STEAKS, EACH CUT ½ INCH THICK (ABOUT 2 POUNDS TOTAL)

1 SMALL TOMATO, COARSELY CHOPPED, PLUS 3 MEDIUM TOMATOES, THINLY SLICED

3 TABLESPOONS CHOPPED PARSLEY (OPTIONAL)

Preheat the grill. Spray the grill with nonstick cooking spray.

In a small bowl, stir together the mustard, lemon juice, olive oil, Parmesan, basil, salt, and pepper.

Place the swordfish steaks on the grill and brush them lightly with some of the basil basting sauce. Grill the steaks 4 inches from the heat until opaque on top, 3 to 4 minutes.

Meanwhile, add the choped tomato and the parsley to the remaining basting sauce.

Turn the fish steaks and spoon the tomato-basil basting sauce over them. Grill until the fish is lightly colored, firm to the touch, and just flakes when tested with a fork, 3 to 4 minutes longer.

Arrange the sliced tomatoes on a platter and top them with the grilled swordfish steaks. Spoon any remaining sauce over the steaks, scatter the chopped basil leaves over all, and serve immediately.

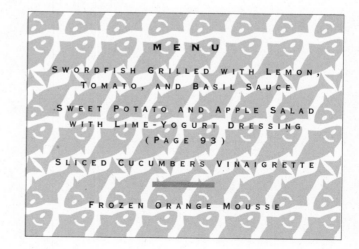

MENU

SWORDFISH GRILLED WITH LEMON, TOMATO, AND BASIL SAUCE

SWEET POTATO AND APPLE SALAD WITH LIME-YOGURT DRESSING (PAGE 93)

SLICED CUCUMBERS VINAIGRETTE

FROZEN ORANGE MOUSSE

SERVES 6

⅓ CUP FRESH LEMON JUICE

½ CUP RED WINE VINEGAR

3 CLOVES GARLIC, CRUSHED

1½ TABLESPOONS SUGAR

¼ TEASPOON SALT

1½ POUNDS SABLEFISH OR WHITEFISH
FILLETS, SKINNED

3 TABLESPOONS BLACK PEPPERCORNS,
CRACKED

¾ CUP FISH STOCK OR CHICKEN STOCK

2 TEASPOONS CHOPPED FRESH THYME
OR ½ TEASPOON DRIED

2 TABLESPOONS COLD UNSALTED BUTTER,
CUT INTO SMALL PIECES

2 THYME SPRIGS, FOR GARNISH

GRILLED SABLEFISH FILLETS WITH BLACK PEPPERCORN CRUST

In a nonreactive baking dish just large enough to hold the fillets in one layer, stir together the lemon juice, vinegar, garlic, sugar, and salt. Add the sablefish fillets, turn to coat them with the marinade, and let them marinate, covered, in the refrigerator for at least 4 hours, turning them after 2 hours.

Preheat the grill. Spray the grill with nonstick cooking spray.

Remove the fillets from the marinade and pat them dry with paper towels. Sprinkle half of the cracked pepper over the fillets and press the pepper firmly into the flesh with your fingertips. Turn the fillets over and coat them with the remaining black pepper in the same manner.

Grill the fillets 4 inches from the heat for 6 minutes. Gently turn the fillets over and grill them until the flesh just flakes, about 6 minutes more.

While the fish is cooking, strain the marinade into a small nonreactive saucepan and add the stock and thyme. Cook the mixture over medium heat until it is reduced to about ½ cup, about 5 minutes.

When the fillets are cooked, transfer them to a heated platter. Whisk the butter, one piece at a time, into the sauce, whisking until it is completely incorporated before adding the next. Pour the butter sauce over the fillets, garnish with the thyme sprigs, and serve at once.

SEA BASS GRILLED WITH SAFFRON, THYME, AND LEMON

ONE 5-POUND SEA BASS,
CLEANED AND SCALED

1 TEASPOON EXTRA-VIRGIN OLIVE OIL

½ TEASPOON GROUND SAFFRON

½ TEASPOON SALT

FRESHLY GROUND BLACK PEPPER,
TO TASTE

1 LEMON, SLICED

1 LARGE BUNCH FRESH THYME,
STALKS TRIMMED

TIED BUNDLES OF CHIVES, FOR GARNISH

SLICES OF LEMON AND WEDGES OF LIME,
FOR GARNISH

Preheat the grill. Spray a grilling basket with nonstick cooking spray.

Rinse the sea bass under cold running water and pat it dry with paper towels. With a sharp knife, make four ¼-inch-deep slashes in the flesh on both sides of the fish. Using a small pastry brush, spread a little of the olive oil on each slash, then paint with some of the saffron. Place the fish in the prepared grilling basket, and season the cavity with the salt and pepper. Place the lemon slices and the bunch of thyme in the cavity, arranging them so that the natural shape of the fish is retained. Close the grilling basket.

Grill the sea bass 4 to 5 inches from the heat for 20 minutes on each side, or until it is firm to the touch. Transfer the fish to a large heated platter and garnish it with the chive bundles, lemon slices, and lime wedges.

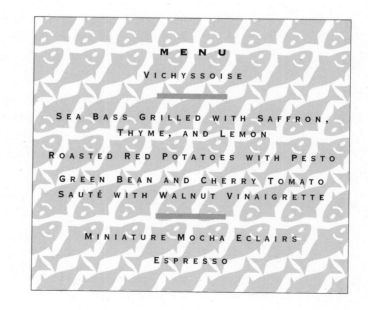

MENU

VICHYSSOISE

SEA BASS GRILLED WITH SAFFRON,
THYME, AND LEMON

ROASTED RED POTATOES WITH PESTO

GREEN BEAN AND CHERRY TOMATO
SAUTÉ WITH WALNUT VINAIGRETTE

MINIATURE MOCHA ECLAIRS

ESPRESSO

GRILLED TUNA STEAKS WITH SCALLION-YOGURT SAUCE

THREE 8-OUNCE TUNA STEAKS

8 SCALLIONS, CHOPPED

2-INCH PIECE FRESH GINGER, UNPEELED AND GRATED

4 CLOVES GARLIC

1 LARGE ONION, CHOPPED

JUICE OF 1 LIME

¼ CUP WHITE WINE VINEGAR

2 TABLESPOONS EXTRA-VIRGIN OLIVE OIL

1 TEASPOON FINELY CRUSHED BLACK PEPPERCORNS

⅛ TEASPOON SALT

¾ CUP PLAIN LOWFAT YOGURT

SLICES OF LIME, FOR GARNISH

Cut the tuna steaks in half and, if necessary, remove the bone from the middle of each steak. Place the fish pieces in a shallow nonreactive dish.

In a food processor or blender, combine the scallions, ginger, garlic, and onion. Add the lime juice, vinegar, and oil, and process to a smooth purée. Stir in the peppercorns and salt.

Pour two-thirds of the mixture over the fish pieces, coating them evenly; reserve the remaining purée for use in the sauce. Cover the fish pieces and let them marinate in the refrigerator for at least 3 hours, or up to 12 hours. Remove the fish pieces from the refrigerator at least 1 hour before they are to be grilled to allow them to reach room temperature.

Before grilling, soak 6 bamboo skewers in water for 10 minutes. Thread one skewer through each piece of tuna about 1 inch from the straight, cut edge; this will keep the steak flat as it cooks. Grill the tuna 4 to 5 inches from the heat for 5 to 6 minutes, turn, and grill 5 to 6 minutes more, until lightly browned and cooked through.

While the tuna is grilling, in a serving bowl or sauceboat, combine the yogurt with the remaining scallion purée to make a sauce.

Transfer the tuna pieces to a heated platter and remove the bamboo skewers. Garnish the tuna with lime slices and serve the scallion-yogurt sauce on the side.

GRILLED HALIBUT WITH AVOCADO AND PEPPER SALAD

3 QUARTER-SIZE SLICES, EACH ¼ INCH
THICK, FRESH GINGER, UNPEELED

2 CLOVES GARLIC

¼ CUP (PACKED) PARSLEY SPRIGS

2 MEDIUM SHALLOTS OR 1 SMALL ONION

¼ CUP FRESH LEMON JUICE

4 HALIBUT STEAKS (ABOUT
2¼ POUNDS TOTAL)

2 TABLESPOONS UNSALTED BUTTER,
MELTED

1 RIPE AVOCADO, PEELED AND CUBED

1 LARGE RED BELL PEPPER, SEEDED,
DERIBBED, AND DICED

2 TABLESPOONS REDUCED-SODIUM
SOY SAUCE

1 TABLESPOON OLIVE OR OTHER
VEGETABLE OIL

3 TABLESPOONS CREAMY PEANUT BUTTER

2 TEASPOONS HONEY

1 TABLESPOON GRATED LEMON ZEST

¼ TEASPOON FRESHLY GROUND
BLACK PEPPER

Preheat the grill. Spray the grill with nonstick cooking spray.

In a food processor, mince the ginger. Add the garlic and parsley and mince. Add the shallots and finely chop. In a small saucepan or skillet, combine the ginger-shallot mixture with the lemon juice and bring to a boil over medium-high heat. Reduce the heat to low and simmer, uncovered, for 5 minutes. Remove the pan from the heat and set the dressing aside to cool slightly.

Brush the halibut steaks with the melted butter and arrange them on the grill.

Grill the steaks 4 to 5 inches from the heat for about 5 minutes. Turn the steaks and grill them for 4 minutes more, or until the flesh just flakes when tested with the tip of a sharp knife. Remove the fish steaks to a heated plate and keep them warm while you make the salad.

Meanwhile, combine the avocado with the bell pepper. To the reserved dressing mixture, add the soy sauce, olive oil, peanut butter, honey, lemon zest, and black pepper, and stir until completely combined and smooth.

Divide the avocado and bell pepper mixture among 4 slightly heated dinner plates. Place a halibut steak on each plate, and drizzle the dressing over all. Serve at once.

GRILLED HALIBUT WITH AVOCADO AND PEPPER SALAD

GRILLED RED SNAPPER WITH RED PEPPER-CREAM SAUCE

GRILLED RED SNAPPER WITH RED PEPPER-CREAM SAUCE

½ SMALL RED BELL PEPPER, SEEDED AND DERIBBED

½ SMALL ONION

1 CLOVE GARLIC, PEELED

¼ CUP WATER

2 TABLESPOONS DISTILLED WHITE VINEGAR

3 TABLESPOONS CREAM CHEESE (HALF A 3-OUNCE PACKAGE), SOFTENED

1 TABLESPOON TOMATO PASTE

1 TABLESPOON PLAIN LOWFAT YOGURT

1 TEASPOON CHILI POWDER

¼ TEASPOON SALT

PINCH OF FRESHLY GROUND BLACK PEPPER

4 RED SNAPPER FILLETS (ABOUT 1¼ POUNDS TOTAL) OR OTHER FIRM-FLESHED WHITE FISH

2 TABLESPOONS CHOPPED CHIVES OR SCALLION GREENS

Preheat the grill. Spray the grill with nonstick cooking spray.

Meanwhile, in a small saucepan, combine the bell pepper, onion, and garlic with the water and vinegar. Bring the mixture to a boil over medium-high heat, reduce the heat to medium-low, and cover. Simmer until the vegetables are tender, about 10 minutes.

In a food processor, blend the cream cheese, tomato paste, and yogurt.

Drain the vegetables, add them to the food processor, and process until smooth. Blend in the chili powder, salt, and black pepper.

Grill the red snapper fillets 4 inches from the heat until lightly colored, firm to the touch, and the flesh just flakes when tested with a fork, 4 to 5 minutes. Transfer the fish to a heated platter and top each fillet with some of the pepper-cream sauce. Sprinkle with the chopped chives or scallion greens.

MENU

GRILLED RED SNAPPER WITH RED PEPPER-CREAM SAUCE

BROCCOLI-BELL PEPPER SAUTÉ

ORANGE AND RADISH SALAD WITH CORIANDER SEED DRESSING (PAGE 118)

STRAWBERRIES WITH MARSALA AND HEAVY CREAM

SERVES 4

2 TABLESPOONS VEGETABLE OIL

2 TABLESPOONS FINELY
CHOPPED SHALLOT

2 TABLESPOONS CHOPPED FRESH
TARRAGON OR 2 TEASPOONS DRIED

½ CUP BOTTLED CLAM JUICE

¼ CUP UNSWEETENED APPLE JUICE

1 ½ TEASPOONS CORNSTARCH BLENDED
WITH 1 TABLESPOON COLD WATER

¼ TEASPOON SALT

FRESHLY GROUND BLACK PEPPER

ONE 1 ½-POUND SWORDFISH STEAK,
SHARK STEAK, OR TUNA STEAK, TRIMMED
AND CUT INTO 4 EQUAL PIECES

1 RED APPLE, QUARTERED, CORED, AND
CUT INTO THIN WEDGES

1 YELLOW APPLE, QUARTERED, CORED,
AND CUT INTO THIN WEDGES

GRILLED SWORDFISH IN APPLE-TARRAGON SAUCE

Preheat the grill.

In a saucepan, heat 1 tablespoon of the oil over medium heat; add the shallot, and cook until it is translucent, 1 to 2 minutes. Add the tarragon, clam juice, apple juice, cornstarch mixture, ⅛ teaspoon of the salt, and pepper to taste. Whisking constantly, bring the mixture to a boil and let it thicken. Reduce the heat to low and simmer the sauce for 2 to 3 minutes; set the pan aside.

Season the fish steaks with the remaining ⅛ teaspoon salt and a generous grinding of pepper. Brush the steaks with the remaining 1 tablespoon oil. Grill the steaks 4 to 5 inches from the heat until the flesh is opaque when tested with the tip of a knife, 3 to 4 minutes per side.

While the steaks are grilling, reheat the sauce over low heat.

Transfer the swordfish steaks to a heated platter and pour the warm apple-tarragon sauce over them. Garnish the platter with the apples slices and serve immediately.

MENU

GRILLED VEGETABLE KEBABS
(PAGE 89)

GRILLED SWORDFISH IN
APPLE-TARRAGON SAUCE

ROSEMARY-ROASTED NEW POTATOES

TOSSED GREENS SALAD

APRICOT-PEACH CRISP

GRILLED REDFISH WITH CAPER, BELL PEPPER, AND PIMIENTO SAUCE

4 TABLESPOONS UNSALTED BUTTER, CUT INTO ½-INCH BITS, PLUS 2 TABLESPOONS UNSALTED BUTTER, MELTED

½ CUP FINELY CHOPPED ONION

1 TEASPOON FINELY CHOPPED GARLIC

½ CUP BOTTLED CLAM JUICE

¼ CUP FINELY CHOPPED GREEN BELL PEPPER

¼ CUP FINELY CHOPPED PIMIENTO

1 TABLESPOON DRAINED CAPERS

2 TEASPOONS TARRAGON VINEGAR

1 ½ TEASPOONS WORCESTERSHIRE SAUCE

¼ TEASPOON GROUND RED PEPPER

½ TEASPOON SALT

1 TABLESPOON FINELY CHOPPED PARSLEY, PREFERABLY FLAT-LEAF, PLUS ADDITIONAL SPRIGS, FOR GARNISH

SIX 6-OUNCE REDFISH FILLETS, EACH CUT ABOUT ¾ INCH THICK, SKINNED

In a heavy 8- to 10-inch skillet, melt the 4 tablespoons butter pieces over medium heat. When the foam begins to subside, add the onion and garlic and cook, stirring frequently, until they are soft and translucent but not brown, about 5 minutes.

Add the clam juice, bell pepper, pimiento, capers, vinegar, Worcestershire sauce, red pepper, and salt. Stirring constantly, bring to a boil over high heat. Reduce the heat to low and simmer the sauce, partially covered, until it thickens slightly, about 10 minutes.

Remove the skillet from the heat, stir in the parsley, and taste for seasoning. Cover the skillet and keep the sauce warm.

Preheat the grill.

Brush the redfish fillets on both sides with the 2 tablespoons melted butter. Grill the fillets about 5 inches from the heat, turning them, for 15 minutes, or until the flesh flakes easily when tested with a fork.

Transfer the fillets to a heated platter, garnish with the parsley sprigs, and pour the sauce over all. Serve at once.

GRILLED SWORDFISH AND VEGETABLE SKEWERS WITH GARLIC-LIME MARINADE

1 LARGE OR 2 SMALL LIMES

4 TABLESPOONS OLIVE OR OTHER VEGETABLE OIL

2 TABLESPOONS TOMATO PASTE

2 TEASPOONS DRY MUSTARD

4 CLOVES GARLIC, MINCED OR CRUSHED THROUGH A PRESS

¾ TEASPOON SALT

½ TEASPOON SUGAR

½ TEASPOON FRESHLY GROUND BLACK PEPPER

1 POUND SWORDFISH

1 LARGE RED ONION

1 LARGE YELLOW OR GREEN BELL PEPPER

8 CHERRY TOMATOES

Preheat the grill.

Grate the lime zest and measure out 2 teaspoons. Juice the lime and measure out 3 tablespoons.

In a small bowl, combine the lime zest, lime juice, oil, tomato paste, dry mustard, garlic, salt, sugar, and pepper; set the basting mixture aside.

Cut the swordfish into 24 equal pieces. Cut the onion in half and then cut each half into quarters. Halve the bell pepper, seed and derib it, then cut it into 16 pieces, each about 1 inch square.

Dividing equally, and alternating them, thread the swordfish, onion, bell pepper, and cherry tomatoes onto eight 10-inch metal skewers.

Place the skewers on the grill and brush with half the basting mixture. Grill the skewers 4 inches from the heat for 5 minutes. Turn them, brush with the remaining basting mixture, and grill until the fish is lightly colored, firm to the touch, and cooked through, about 5 minutes more.

Arrange 2 skewers on each of 4 heated dinner plates and serve at once.

GRILLED TUNA STEAKS WITH TOMATO AND GREEN OLIVE SALAD

¼ CUP OLIVE OIL

2 TABLESPOONS FRESH LEMON JUICE

1 TABLESPOON CAPERS

1 TEASPOON FINELY CHOPPED GARLIC

1 TEASPOON FINELY CHOPPED FRESH ROSEMARY OR ½ TEASPOON DRIED

½ TEASPOON SALT

FRESHLY GROUND BLACK PEPPER

4 TUNA STEAKS, CUT ½ TO ¾ INCH THICK

2 MEDIUM TOMATOES, PEELED AND SEEDED

⅓ CUP PIMIENTO-STUFFED OLIVES, HALVED

1½ TABLESPOONS BALSAMIC VINEGAR

1 LEMON CUT LENGTHWISE INTO QUARTERS, FOR GARNISH

Preheat the grill.

In a nonreactive dish just large enough to hold the tuna steaks in one layer, combine the olive oil, lemon juice, capers, garlic, rosemary, salt, and a few grindings of pepper. Add the steaks and let them marinate, covered, at room temperature, turning them every 10 minutes, for about 30 minutes.

Dice the tomatoes and combine them in a bowl with the olives and vinegar. Season with salt and pepper to taste.

Remove the tuna steaks from the marinade, reserving it, and arrange them on the grill. Grill the tuna steaks 4 to 5 inches from the heat for about 4 minutes, or until they pale at the edges and are seared on the bottom. Turn them, brush the steaks generously with the reserved marinade, and grill them for 4 minutes more, or until they are firm to the touch. Transfer the steaks to a heated platter, spread the tomato-olive salad over them, and garnish with the lemon wedges.

MENU

GRILLED TUNA STEAKS WITH TOMATO AND GREEN OLIVE SALAD

ROASTED HERBED CORN ON THE COB (PAGE 90)

GRILLED CUMIN-RUBBED EGGPLANT ROUNDS

ALMOND MACAROONS

GRILLED WHOLE BLUEFISH WITH SPINACH AND MUSHROOM STUFFING

2 TABLESPOONS FRUITY OLIVE OIL

1 RED BELL PEPPER, CUT INTO ½-INCH DICE

1 ONION, DICED

2 MEDIUM TOMATOES, SEEDED AND CUT INTO ½-INCH DICE

¼ POUND MUSHROOMS, THINLY SLICED

¾ TEASPOON MINCED GARLIC

JUICE OF 1 LEMON

1 TEASPOON CHOPPED PARSLEY

1 TEASPOON CHOPPED FRESH DILL

1½ TEASPOONS CHOPPED FRESH BASIL OR ½ TEASPOON DRIED

¾ POUND SPINACH, STEMMED AND CUT INTO 1-INCH-WIDE STRIPS

½ CUP DRY WHITE WINE

5 SLICES WHITE OR WHOLE WHEAT BREAD (ABOUT 4 OUNCES)

1 EGG, LIGHTLY BEATEN

SALT AND FRESHLY GROUND BLACK PEPPER

ONE 3-POUND BLUEFISH, CLEANED, WITH HEAD AND TAIL REMOVED

WATERCRESS SPRIGS, CHERRY TOMATOES, AND LEMON SLICES, FOR GARNISH

Preheat the grill. Spray a grilling basket with nonstick cooking spray.

In a large nonreactive skillet, heat the olive oil over medium-high heat until hot but not smoking. Add the bell pepper, onion, tomatoes, mushrooms, garlic, lemon juice, parsley, dill, and basil and sauté the mixture, stirring frequently until slightly softened, about 5 minutes.

Add the spinach and wine, and stir to combine. Cook, stirring frequently, until the spinach is wilted but still bright green, about 5 minutes. Set a strainer over a medium bowl. Turn the spinach mixture into the strainer and drain thoroughly; reserve the strained liquid.

Tear the bread into coarse medium-sized pieces and combine it in a bowl with the drained spinach mixture; toss to combine. Add the beaten egg and stir it in until incorporated. Season generously with salt and black pepper.

Season the bluefish cavity lightly with salt and black pepper, then fill it with the stuffing, packing it in loosely. (Do not overfill; the stuffing will expand during cooking.) Tie the fish securely but not too tightly closed with kitchen string in several places, or use strips of foil in place of the string.

Place the stuffed bluefish in the grilling basket and close the basket. Grill the fish 4 inches from the heat, basting it with the reserved vegetable liquid and turning it frequently, for about 25 minutes, or until the flesh just flakes when tested with a fork.

Remove the grilling basket from the grill. Open the basket, invert a heated platter over the side of the basket holding the fish, and invert the basket so that the fish drops gently onto the platter. Remove the strings. Garnish the platter with the watercress sprigs, cherry tomatoes, and lemon slices and serve at once.

4 TABLESPOONS EXTRA-VIRGIN OLIVE OIL

⅓ CUP FRESH LIME JUICE

1 TABLESPOON GIN

¼ TEASPOON SALT

FRESHLY GROUND BLACK PEPPER,
TO TASTE

1½ POUNDS SHARK FILLET, SKINNED

16 SMALL BOILING ONIONS, COOKED IN
BOILING WATER FOR 8 TO 10 MINUTES,
UNTIL JUST TENDER

1 ORANGE BELL PEPPER, SEEDED,
DERIBBED, AND CUT INTO 8 PIECES,
EACH 1 INCH IN SIZE

1 YELLOW BELL PEPPER, SEEDED,
DERIBBED, AND CUT INTO 8 PIECES,
EACH 1 INCH IN SIZE

BAMBOO LEAVES, FOR GARNISHING
THE PLATTER (OPTIONAL)

WEDGES OF LIME AND LEMON,
FOR GARNISH

SHARK, ONION, AND PEPPER BROCHETTES

In a large nonreactive baking dish, combine 3 tablespoons of the olive oil with the lime juice, gin, salt, and pepper. Cut the shark into 24 cubes, add them to the marinade, and turn to coat them completely. Arrange the cubes in a single layer, cover, and place the dish in the refrigerator for at least 24 hours. Turn the cubes over from time to time while they marinate.

Preheat the grill.

Divide the shark cubes, onions, and pieces of orange and yellow pepper into 8 equal portions. Thread each portion onto a 10-inch metal skewer, alternating the ingredients, then brush the skewers with the remaining olive oil.

Arrange the skewers on the grill 4 or 5 inches from the heat and grill them for about 10 minutes in all, turning them after 5 minutes to cook evenly on both sides. When done, the shark will be firm to the touch and the onions and peppers will be lightly charred. Serve the skewers on a platter covered with bamboo leaves, if desired. Garnish with the lime and lemon wedges.

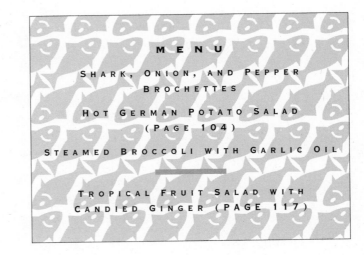

MENU

SHARK, ONION, AND PEPPER
BROCHETTES

HOT GERMAN POTATO SALAD
(PAGE 104)

STEAMED BROCCOLI WITH GARLIC OIL

TROPICAL FRUIT SALAD WITH
CANDIED GINGER (PAGE 117)

3 TABLESPOONS OLIVE OR OTHER
VEGETABLE OIL

2 TABLESPOONS DIJON MUSTARD

2 TABLESPOONS FRESH LEMON JUICE

2 TEASPOONS GRATED LEMON ZEST

3 CLOVES GARLIC, MINCED OR CRUSHED
THROUGH A PRESS

½ TEASPOON SALT

¼ TEASPOON FRESHLY GROUND
BLACK PEPPER

¼ CUP (PACKED) FRESH BASIL LEAVES

¼ CUP (PACKED) FRESH DILL SPRIGS

¼ CUP (PACKED) PARSLEY SPRIGS

¼ POUND SPINACH, TOUGH STEMS
REMOVED

¼ CUP PLAIN LOWFAT YOGURT

FOUR 8-OUNCE SALMON STEAKS

GRILLED SALMON WITH GREEN SAUCE

Preheat the grill. Spray the grill with nonstick cooking spray.

In a small bowl, blend the oil, mustard, lemon juice, lemon zest, garlic, salt, and pepper. Measure out 1 tablespoon of the flavored oil to use as a basting mixture for the salmon and set aside.

In a food processor, mince the basil, dill, and parsley. Add the spinach and purée. Add the yogurt and blend. With the machine running, drizzle in the flavored oil until the mixture thickens to mayonnaise consistency. Pour the sauce into a serving bowl, cover, and refrigerate until ready to serve.

Lightly brush the salmon steaks with half of the basting mixture. Grill the salmon steaks 4 inches from the heat for 6 minutes. Turn the steaks, brush them with the remaining basting mixture, and grill until lightly colored and the flesh just flakes when tested with a fork, 4 to 6 minutes more, depending upon the thickness of the steaks. Transfer the salmon steaks to a heated platter and serve with the green sauce on the side.

MENU

MINIATURE QUICHE LORRAINES

GRILLED SALMON WITH
GREEN SAUCE

MESCLUN SALAD WITH
PEPPERS AND TOMATOES

HERBED GARLIC TOAST

BROWN SUGAR SHORTBREAD

GRILLED SALMON WITH GREEN SAUCE

GRILLED SOLE FILLETS WITH CUCUMBER-DILL SAUCE

(PAGE 65)

GRILLED SALMON WITH LEMON MAYONNAISE

(PAGE 64)

SEA BASS GRILLED WITH LIME-GINGER SAUCE

SERVES 4

1 LIME

3 QUARTER-SIZE SLICES, ¼ INCH THICK,
FRESH GINGER, UNPEELED

3 TABLESPOONS REDUCED-SODIUM OR
REGULAR SOY SAUCE

1 TABLESPOON VEGETABLE OIL

2 CLOVES GARLIC, MINCED OR CRUSHED
THROUGH A PRESS

¼ TEASPOON RED PEPPER FLAKES

¼ TEASPOON FRESHLY GROUND
BLACK PEPPER

1 ¼ POUNDS SEA BASS FILLETS OR OTHER
FIRM-FLESHED WHITE FISH,
SUCH AS SCROD

SEA BASS GRILLED WITH LIME-GINGER SAUCE

Preheat the grill. Spray the grill with nonstick cooking spray.

Grate the lime to yield about 2 teaspoons zest, then juice it. Cut the ginger into thin slivers.

In a small bowl, combine the lime zest, lime juice, ginger, soy sauce, oil, garlic, red pepper flakes, and black pepper.

Place the sea bass fillets, skin-side up, on the grill and drizzle them evenly with some of the lime-ginger sauce. Grill the fish 4 inches from the heat for about 5 minutes. Turn the fish, baste it with some of the lime-ginger sauce, and grill it for 4 to 5 minutes more, or until the flesh is opaque and just flakes when tested with a fork. Transfer the fish to heated platter and serve the remaining sauce on the side.

MENU

GAZPACHO WITH
GARLIC CROUTONS

SEA BASS GRILLED WITH
LIME-GINGER SAUCE
STEAMED SNOW PEAS

PEAR, FENNEL, AND WATERCRESS
SALAD WITH TART LEMON
DRESSING (PAGE 119)

FRESH RASPBERRIES WITH
CREME FRAICHE

SESAME MONKFISH, SHRIMP, AND SCALLOP KEBABS

½ LEMON

1 TABLESPOON VEGETABLE OIL

1 CLOVE GARLIC, CRUSHED

⅛ TEASPOON SALT

FRESHLY GROUND BLACK PEPPER

¾ POUND MONKFISH FILLETS

1 TEASPOON CORNSTARCH

1 TABLESPOON CHOPPED MIXED FRESH HERBS, SUCH AS BASIL, PARSLEY, AND CHIVES

1 TABLESPOON SESAME SEEDS, TOASTED

4 LARGE SHRIMP (WITH THE HEADS ON, IF POSSIBLE)

8 LARGE SEA SCALLOPS

SHREDDED LETTUCE, FOR GARNISH

Grate the zest from the ½ lemon. Juice the lemon and measure out 1 tablespoon.

In a ceramic or glass bowl, combine the lemon zest and lemon juice with ½ cup of the wine, the oil, garlic, salt, and some pepper. Pour half of the mixture into a small, nonreactive saucepan and set aside.

Cut the monkfish into 12 equal pieces and add to the wine mixture in the bowl. Turn the pieces over in the marinade to coat them thoroughly. Cover the bowl and place it in the refrigerator for 1 to 2 hours.

Preheat the grill.

Add the remaining ½ cup wine to the saucepan. Blend the cornstarch to a smooth paste with a little cold water. Stir the paste into the liquid in the pan and heat it slowly, stirring constantly, until it boils and thickens. Remove the pan from the heat and stir in the mixed herbs and the sesame seeds. Cover the pan and set it over very low heat to keep the sauce hot while the kebabs grill.

Lightly oil four 10-inch metal skewers. Drain the monkfish and thread the pieces onto the skewers, alternating them with the shrimp and scallops.

Grill the kebabs 4 to 5 inches from the heat for 3 to 5 minutes, turn the kebabs gently, and grill for 3 to 5 minutes more. The fish is done when it is firm to the touch and the shellfish is lightly golden.

Spread the shredded lettuce on a large platter and pour the sauce into a warmed pitcher. Arrange the kebabs on the lettuce and serve them immediately, accompanied by the sauce.

3 CUPS DRY WHITE WINE

½ CUP FRESH LEMON JUICE

½ CUP VEGETABLE OIL

¼ CUP GRATED ONION

1 TABLESPOON SALT

1½ TEASPOONS GROUND WHITE PEPPER

24 LOBSTER TAILS, MEAT REMOVED AND
CUT INTO 2-INCH PIECES

36 MEDIUM-TO-LARGE MUSHROOM CAPS

½ CUP BRANDY, HEATED

FLAMBEED LOBSTER AND MUSHROOM KEBABS

In a glass bowl, combine the wine, lemon juice, oil, onion, salt, and pepper. Marinate the lobster in the mixture overnight in the refrigerator, turning a few times. With a slotted spoon, remove the lobster from the marinade, reserving it.

Preheat the grill.

Put the mushroom caps in the marinade, and let them stand for 10 minutes.

Alternating the lobster and mushroom caps, thread the pieces onto 12 oiled skewers, starting and ending with lobster. Grill the skewers 4 to 5 inches from the heat, turning them, for about 10 minutes, or until the lobsdter is firm to the touch and opaque throughout.

Arrange the skewers on a heated platter. Pour the warm brandy over them, carefully set it aflame, and present the platter flaming.

MENU

SMOKED TROUT WITH
HORSERADISH CREAM

FLAMBÉED LOBSTER AND
MUSHROOM KEBABS

GREEN AND WHITE RICE SALAD WITH
WALNUT VINAIGRETTE (PAGE 58)

APRICOT TART

CHOCOLATE TRUFFLES

2 POUNDS LARGE SHRIMP,
16 OR 18 TO THE POUND

1 CUP OLIVE OIL

2 TABLESPOONS RED WINE VINEGAR

1 TABLESPOON TOMATO PASTE

1 TABLESPOON DRIED OREGANO

1 TO 2 TABLESPOONS MINCED GARLIC

3 TABLESPOONS FINELY
CHOPPED PARSLEY

1 TEASPOON SALT

FRESHLY GROUND BLACK PEPPER

LEMON WEDGES, FOR GARNISH

BARBECUED GARLIC SHRIMP

Shell each shrimp carefully by breaking off the shell just above the point where it joins the tail, but don't remove the tail. With a small knife, make a shallow incision down the back of the shrimp and lift out the intestinal vein. Wash the shrimp thoroughly in cold water and pat them dry with paper towels.

In a large bowl, combine the olive oil, vinegar, tomato paste, oregano, garlic, parsley, salt and a few grindings of black pepper. Drop in the shrimp and stir gently to coat each well with marinade. Let the shrimp marinate at room temperature for about 2 hours, stirring gently every ½ hour or so.

Preheat the grill.

Reserving the marinade, arrange the shrimp in one layer in a large grilling basket; close the basket. Grill the shrimp 4 to 5 inches from the heat for 3 minutes, then baste with the marinade. Grill for 2 minutes. Turn the shrimp, baste them with the marinade, and grill for 3 minutes, or until the shrimp are cooked through, but still moist, lightly colored, and firm to the touch. Be careful not to overcook.

Serve the barbecued shrimp on a large heated platter, garnished with the lemon wedges and with the remaining marinade, heated, on the side. The shrimp are customarily eaten by holding one by the tail and dipping it into the marinade.

2 TABLESPOONS FRESH LEMON JUICE

1 TEASPOON SALT

¼ TEASPOON FRESHLY GROUND
BLACK PEPPER

1 POUND SEA SCALLOPS, HALVED OR
QUARTERED (IF LARGE)

8 SLICES LEAN BACON

1 STICK (½ CUP) UNSALTED BUTTER,
MELTED AND COOLED

1 LEMON, CUT LENGTHWISE INTO
QUARTERS

GRILLED SKEWERED SCALLOPS WITH BACON

Preheat the grill.

Combine the lemon juice, salt, and pepper in a small bowl and mix well. Drop in the scallops and stir them to coat evenly.

Thread the scallops and bacon onto four 10-inch metal skewers, looping the bacon slices up and down to weave them over and under the scallops. Push the scallops compactly together. With a pastry brush, thoroughly coat the scallops with a few spoonfuls of the melted butter.

Grill the skewers 4 inches from the heat, turning them and basting the scallops frequently with the remaining melted butter, for about 4 to 5 minutes. The scallops are done when they are opaque and firm to the touch, and the bacon is brown but not charred.

Slide the scallops and bacon off the skewers onto a heated platter. Serve at once, accompanied with the lemon quarters.

MENU

CHILLED CREAM OF CARROT SOUP

GRILLED SKEWERED SCALLOPS
WITH BACON

MARINATED CORN SALAD (PAGE 107)

WILTED SPINACH SALAD WITH
SESAME VINAIGRETTE

GRILLED PINEAPPLE ROUNDS
WITH RUM BUTTER

GRILLED SPANISH MACKEREL WITH ANCHOVY BUTTER

1 STICK (½ CUP) UNSALTED BUTTER, CUT INTO PIECES

2 TABLESPOONS FRESH LIME JUICE

1 TEASPOON ANCHOVY PASTE

¼ TEASPOON GROUND RED PEPPER, OR TO TASTE

½ TEASPOON SALT, OR TO TASTE

4 SPANISH MACKEREL FILLETS, EACH ABOUT 6 OUNCES, SKINNED

1 LIME, CUT LENGTHWISE INTO 4 OR 8 WEDGES

Preheat the grill. Spray a grilling basket with nonstick cooking spray.

In a small saucepan, melt the butter over medium heat. Remove the pan from the heat and stir in the lime juice, anchovy paste, red pepper, and salt. Set the butter sauce aside.

Arrange the mackerel fillets side by side on the grill, and brush them with about 2 tablespoons of the butter sauce. Grill them 4 to 5 inches from the heat, turning them once and brushing them with 2 more tablespoons butter sauce, for 4 to 5 minutes. The mackerel is done when the fillets are golden brown and the flesh feels firm to the touch. Transfer the fillets to a heated platter, arrange the lime wedges around the fish, and serve the remaining anchovy butter in a heated serving bowl on the side.

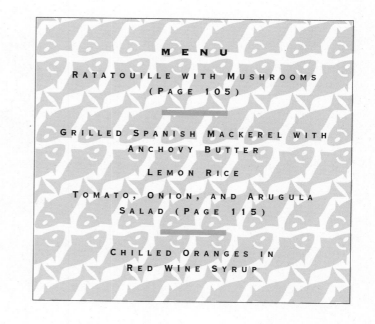

MENU

RATATOUILLE WITH MUSHROOMS
(PAGE 105)

GRILLED SPANISH MACKEREL WITH
ANCHOVY BUTTER

LEMON RICE

TOMATO, ONION, AND ARUGULA
SALAD (PAGE 115)

CHILLED ORANGES IN
RED WINE SYRUP

GRILLED STUFFED COHO SALMON

1½ CUPS DRY WHITE WINE

½ CUP FRESH LEMON JUICE, PLUS THE PEEL OF ½ LEMON, CUT INTO JULIENNE STRIPS

½ CUP VEGETABLE OIL

1 ONION, THINLY SLICED

3 CLOVES GARLIC, CRUSHED

½ CUP CHOPPED PARSLEY

1 TEASPOON GROUND GINGER

½ TEASPOON DRIED THYME

¼ TEASPOON HOT PEPPER SAUCE

1 TEASPOON SALT

¼ TEASPOON FRESHLY GROUND BLACK PEPPER

ONE 5- TO 5½-POUND COHO SALMON, CLEANED, WITH HEAD AND TAIL LEFT ON

1 CUP COOKED RICE, COOLED

¼ CUP FINELY CHOPPED SCALLIONS, INCLUDING 2 INCHES OF GREEN TOPS

JULIENNE STRIPS OF RED AND GREEN BELL PEPPER AND THIN LEMON SLICES, FOR GARNISH

In a small nonreactive saucepan, combine the wine, lemon juice, oil, onion, garlic, ¼ cup of the parsley, the ginger, thyme, hot pepper sauce, salt, and pepper and bring to a boil over high heat, stirring occasionally. Pour the marinade into a nonreactive fish poacher or casserole large enough to hold the salmon and set aside to cool to room temperature.

With a sharp knife, score the fish by making 3 or 4 evenly spaced diagonal slits about 4 inches long and ¼ inch deep on both sides of the salmon. Place the salmon in the cool marinade and turn it over to moisten it evenly. Cover the pan and marinate at room temperature for about 3 hours, or in the refrigerator for about 6 hours, turning the fish occasionally.

Preheat the grill. Spray a grilling basket with nonstick cooking spray.

Meanwhile, transfer the salmon to paper towels and pat it dry. Pour the marinade into a pitcher or bowl.

To make the stuffing, combine the cooled rice, scallions, the remaining parsley, and the julienned lemon peel in a small bowl. Blend in ¼ cup of marinade. Set the remaining marinade aside.

Loosely fill the salmon with the stuffing, then close the opening with small skewers and kitchen cord. Place the salmon in the basket and brush it with a few spoonfuls of the reserved marinade. Place the basket on the grill 4 to 5 inches from the heat and grill it, basting it frequently with the remaining marinade, for about 15 minutes on each side, or until delicately browned and when prodded gently with a finger the flesh feels firm to the touch.

Transfer the salmon to a large heated platter and serve at once, garnished with red and green pepper strips and lemon slices.

1 LEMON

½ CUP MAYONNAISE

2 TABLESPOONS CHOPPED PARSLEY

¼ TEASPOON SALT

¼ TEASPOON GROUND WHITE PEPPER

FOUR 5-OUNCE SALMON FILLETS

GRILLED SALMON WITH LEMON MAYONNAISE

Preheat the grill. Spray a grilling basket with nonstick cooking spray.

Grate the lemon to make 1 tablespoon zest, then squeeze the lemon to make 2 tablespoons juice.

In a small bowl, combine the lemon juice, lemon zest, mayonnaise, parsley, salt, and white pepper.

Place the salmon fillets skin-side down on the prepared grilling basket. Spread them with half of the lemon mayonnaise and close the basket. Grill the fish, skin-side down, 4 inches from the heat for 4 minutes; turn them, and grill for about 4 minutes more, until the topping is golden and slightly puffed. Divide the salmon fillets among 4 heated dinner plates and serve the remaining lemon mayonnaise on the side.

MENU

GRILLED PEARS WITH
CRUMBLED ROQUEFORT

GRILLED SALMON WITH
LEMON MAYONNAISE

ROASTED NEW POTATOES
IN ROSEMARY OIL

SHAKER GREEN BEAN SALAD
(PAGE 120)

BUTTERSCOTCH MERINGUE PIE

GRILLED SOLE FILLETS WITH CUCUMBER-DILL SAUCE

1 TABLESPOON UNSALTED BUTTER, MELTED

¼ CUP (PACKED) FRESH DILL SPRIGS OR 1½ TEASPOONS DRIED

½ TEASPOON SALT

½ TEASPOON FRESHLY GROUND BLACK PEPPER

1 CUP PLAIN LOWFAT YOGURT

3 TABLESPOONS FRESH LEMON JUICE

2 TEASPOONS GRATED LEMON ZEST

½ TEASPOON DRY MUSTARD

ONE 2-INCH PIECE OF CUCUMBER, PEELED, SEEDED, AND FINELY CHOPPED

¼ CUP FINELY CHOPPED RED BELL PEPPER

4 SMALL SOLE FILLETS OR OTHER FIRM-FLESHED WHITE FISH (ABOUT 1½ POUNDS TOTAL)

Preheat the grill. Spray a grilling basket with nonstick cooking spray.

In a small bowl, combine the melted butter with 1 tablespoon of the fresh dill (or ½ teaspoon of the dried), ¼ teaspoon of the salt, and ¼ teaspoon of the pepper.

In a serving bowl, combine the yogurt, lemon juice, lemon zest, mustard, the remaining 3 tablespoons fresh dill (or 1 teaspoon dried), the remaining ¼ teaspoon each of salt and pepper. Stir in the cucumber and bell pepper.

Brush the dill butter over the sole fillets and arrange them in the grilling basket; close the basket. Grill the fillets 4 to 5 inches from the heat, turning them once and brushing them with the dill butter again, until the fish just flakes when tested with a fork, about 7 minutes. Divide the sole fillets among heated plates and top each with a generous dollop of cucumber-dill sauce.

MENU

GRILLED SOLE WITH CUCUMBER-DILL SAUCE

ROASTED HERBED POTATO FANS (PAGE 87)

ARUGULA SALAD WITH CUCUMBERS AND TOMATOES

RASPBERRY SORBET

SUGAR COOKIES

1 TABLESPOON DRY MUSTARD

¼ CUP SOY SAUCE

¼ CUP DRY SHERRY

½ CUP CHICKEN BROTH

1 TABLESPOON SUGAR

2 TEASPOONS CORNSTARCH BLENDED
WITH 1 TABLESPOON WATER

FOUR 8-OUNCE STRIPED BASS FILLETS

PARSLEY SPRIGS, FOR GARNISH

STRIPED BASS TERIYAKI

Preheat the grill. Spray the grill with nonstick cooking spray.

In a small bowl, mix the dry mustard with just enough hot water to make a thick paste; set aside for 15 minutes.

In a small saucepan, combine the soy sauce, sherry, chicken broth, and sugar and bring to a simmer over medium heat. Restir the cornstarch mixture, stir it into the saucepan, and cook the mixture over low heat, stirring constantly, until it thickens to a syrupy glaze. Immediately pour the sauce into a dish and set aside.

Place the fillets on the grill, skin-side down, and brush them with about 2 tablespoons of the teriyaki glaze. Grill the fillets 4 to 5 inches from the heat for 6 to 8 minutes, turning them and brushing them three or four times with the remaining glaze, until the flesh feels firm when tested gently with a finger and the flesh flakes when tested with a fork.

Transfer the fish fillets to 4 heated dinner plates. Mix the reserved mustard paste into the remaining glaze, spoon a little over each serving, and garnish each fillet with a parsley sprig. Serve at once.

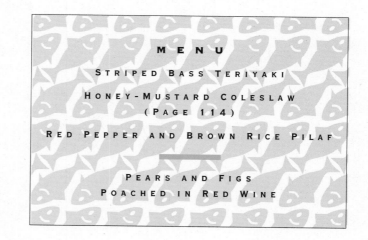

MENU

STRIPED BASS TERIYAKI

HONEY-MUSTARD COLESLAW
(PAGE 114)

RED PEPPER AND BROWN RICE PILAF

PEARS AND FIGS
POACHED IN RED WINE

GRILLED TARRAGON-MARINATED SALMON WITH PEPPERY NEW POTATOES

2 ¼ POUNDS SALMON FILLET, 1 LARGE OR 2 SMALLER PIECES

3 TABLESPOONS CHOPPED FRESH TARRAGON

1 TABLESPOON SALT

2 TABLESPOONS LIGHT BROWN SUGAR

1 TABLESPOON VODKA

1 ½ TEASPOONS CRUSHED BLACK PEPPERCORNS

¾ POUND VERY SMALL NEW POTATOES

1 TEASPOON GRAPE-SEED OR SAFFLOWER OIL

DRIED FENNEL BRANCHES OR SEEDS, TO BURN ON THE COALS (OPTIONAL)

FENNEL LEAVES, FOR GARNISH

Lay the salmon in a large shallow nonreactive dish.

In a small nonreactive dish, mix the chopped tarragon, salt, sugar, vodka, and 1 teaspoon of the crushed black peppercorns. Using the back of a spoon, spread the tarragon marinade all over the flesh side of the salmon. (If you are using two pieces of salmon, sandwich the flesh sides together.) Cover the salmon loosely with a damp cloth, and let it marinate in the refrigerator at least 12 hours, or up to 48 hours.

Preheat the grill. Spray the grill with nonstick cooking spray. Soak 6 bamboo skewers in cold water for 10 minutes, and drain them.

In a large saucepan, cook the new potatoes in boiling water to cover until just tender when tested with a fork, 10 to 15 minutes. Drain and return the potatoes to the saucepan. Add the oil and the remaining crushed peppercorns, and toss the potatoes until they are evenly coated in oil and peppercorns. Thread the potatoes onto the drained, soaked skewers, and set them aside.

Wipe all the marinade off the salmon. Place it, flesh-side down, on the grill 4 to 5 inches from the heat and grill it for 1 minute. Turn the salmon and grill it for 6 to 9 minutes more, until it is almost cooked through but not quite opaque in the center.

After about 3 minutes, place the skewered potatoes on the rack and heat them, turning them frequently, until browned. At the same time, throw the dried fennel twigs or seeds, if you are using them, onto the coals to produce aromatic smoke.

Transfer the grilled salmon to a large heated platter. Remove the potatoes from the skewers and arrange them around the fish; garnish with the fennel leaves. To serve the fish, carve off thin slices, keeping the knife almost parallel with the fillet.

SERVES 4 TO 6

2 TABLESPOONS EXTRA-VIRGIN OLIVE OIL

1 CLOVE GARLIC, CRUSHED

3 MEDIUM TOMATOES, PEELED, SEEDED,
AND CHOPPED

2 TEASPOONS RED WINE VINEGAR

2 TEASPOONS PAPRIKA

1 TEASPOON HOT PEPPER SAUCE

6 OUNCES PIMIENTOS, COARSELY
CHOPPED

1½ POUNDS SQUID, CLEANED AND
SKINNED, TENTACLES REMOVED
BUT RESERVED

48 SMALL MUSHROOM CAPS

GRILLED SQUID WITH HOT PAPRIKA SAUCE

Preheat the grill.

In a large nonreactive skillet, heat the oil over medium heat until hot but not smoking. Add the garlic and tomatoes and cook them, stirring constantly, for 10 minutes. Strain off and discard 1¼ cups of the juice. Add the vinegar to the skillet and simmer the mixture for 3 minutes more. Pour the mixture into a food processor or blender, add the paprika, hot pepper sauce, and chopped pimientos, and process until smooth. Transfer the sauce to a bowl and set it aside.

Cut the body of each squid into 3 or 4 flat pieces and the tentacles into groups of 4. Thread the squid and mushrooms, alternating them, onto twelve 10-inch metal skewers. Grill the skewers 4 to 5 inches from the heat, spreading out the tentacles, for 5 minutes on each side, until the squid is golden brown.

Remove the squid and mushrooms from the skewers to a heated platter and mix together. Serve the hot paprika sauce on the side.

MENU

BRUSHCHETTA

GRILLED SQUID WITH
HOT PAPRIKA SAUCE

GRILLED YELLOW AND GREEN
BELL PEPPERS (PAGE 88)

ROASTED SWEET POTATOES

CHOCOLATE PECAN TARTS

SERVES 4

12 HARD-SHELLED CLAMS

12 OYSTERS

2 MEDIUM-SIZE LOBSTERS (ABOUT
1¼ POUNDS EACH)

1 CUP DRY WHITE WINE

1 TABLESPOON MINCED SHALLOT
OR ONION

PINCH OF SAFFRON THREADS

2 STICKS (1 CUP) BUTTER, CUT INTO
16 TABLESPOONS

SALT AND FRESHLY GROUND
BLACK PEPPER

6 FRESH BASIL LEAVES, CHOPPED

MESQUITE-GRILLED CLAMS, OYSTERS, AND LOBSTERS WITH SAFFRON BUTTER

With a wire brush, scrub the clams and oysters thoroughly, and rinse in several changes of cold water.

Preheat the grill and when the coals are ready, add mesquite chips to flavor the smoke.

Set a sieve over a small saucepan. Using an oyster knife, open each oyster over the sieve, and pour the liquor through the sieve into the pan. Set aside. Loosen each oyster from its bottom shell and discard the bottom shell. Arrange the oysters in their half shells and the clams in a grilling basket; close the basket.

To kill the lobsters, plunge the tip of a knife into the lobster at the point where the body section and tail section meet. Make a small crosswise cut to sever the spinal cord.

Place the grilling basket on the grill about 4 to 5 inches from the heat and grill the clams and oysters, turning them, for 10 to 12 minutes, or until the edges of the oysters are curled and the clams have opened. Add the lobsters to the grill and grill them for 5 to 7 minutes; turn and grill another 4 to 7 minutes, or until the shells have turned bright red.

Meanwhile, bring the oyster liquor to a boil over high heat. Add the wine and shallot, and reduce, stirring occasionally, to about 3 tablespoons, about 15 minutes. Crush the saffron threads and add to the sauce. Reduce the heat to low and start adding the butter to the sauce, 1 tablespoon at a time, whisking until thoroughly incorporated before adding the next. Add salt and pepper to taste. Remove the pan from the heat and stir in the chopped basil. Divide the saffron butter among heated ramekins.

Transfer the lobsters, oysters, and clams to a heated platter and serve the saffron butter on the side.

1 TEASPOON UNSALTED BUTTER

1 SMALL ONION, FINELY CHOPPED

4½ OUNCES FRESH SHAD ROE, BROKEN
INTO PIECES

1 TART APPLE, PEELED AND
FINELY DICED

JUICE OF ½ LEMON

¼ CUP FRESH WHITE BREAD CRUMBS

3 TABLESPOONS ROLLED OATS

1 TABLESPOON APPLE JUICE

2 TABLESPOONS MINCED
FRESH DILL

FRESHLY GROUND BLACK PEPPER

3 HEADS OF BOSTON LETTUCE

6 HERRING (ABOUT 6 OUNCES EACH),
GUTTED AND BONED

SALT

2 TABLESPOONS DIJON MUSTARD

12 SPRIGS OF DILL

LEAF-WRAPPED STUFFED GRILLED HERRING

Preheat the grill. Spray a grilling basket with nonstick cooking spray.

In a nonreactive saucepan, melt the butter over medium heat. Add the onion and cook, stirring, until soft but not browned, about 5 minutes. Add the roe and cook, stirring constantly, until the roe is opaque and broken up, 2 to 3 minutes.

Add the apple and lemon juice to the roe mixture and cook gently until the apple is soft but not mushy, about 5 minutes. Remove the pan from the heat and let the mixture cool slightly.

Mix the bread crumbs with 2 tablespoons of the rolled oats, moisten them with the apple juice and add them to the roe mixture along with the dill and black pepper to taste. Combine well.

Blanch 24 large lettuce leaves in boiling water, a few at a time, for 2 to 3 seconds; drain immediately and refresh under cold running water. Drain the leaves again and set aside.

Season the inside of each herring lightly with salt and pepper. Place equal portions of stuffing inside the body cavity of each fish, then press the sides firmly together. Spread 1 teaspoon of the mustard evenly over the skin of each herring but leaving the head and tail exposed. Then coat each fish in the remaining rolled oats.

For each herring, lay 4 blanched lettuce leaves on the work surface, overlapping them neatly to make an oblong of leaves large enough to wrap around the body of the fish. Top the lettuce with two dill sprigs, and lay the oats-coated herring on the dill. Wrap the lettuce around the fish, leaving the head and tail exposed.

Arrange the lettuce-wrapped herrings, seam-side down, in the grilling basket. Grill the fish for 5 to 10 minutes on each side. Check that the fish are cooked by cutting into the middle of the plumpest herring: If the flesh flakes easily, it is done. Transfer the fish to a heated platter and serve immediately.

SERVES 4

SALMON BARBECUED WITH FENNEL, LEMON, AND ONION

ONE 2½-POUND SALMON FILLET, ABOUT
1¾ INCHES THICK AT THICKEST POINT

3 TABLESPOONS OLIVE OIL

1 MEDIUM ONION, THINLY SLICED

3 LEMONS, CUT INTO SLICES
¼ INCH THICK

6 FRESH FENNEL STALKS WITH GREENS;
OR 1 SMALL BUNCH FRESH DILL;
OR 2 TEASPOONS DRIED DILL COMBINED
WITH ½ TEASPOON FENNEL SEEDS

SALT AND FRESHLY GROUND
BLACK PEPPER

Preheat the grill. Spray a grill basket with nonstick cooking spray.

Coat the salmon fillet on both sides with the olive oil, rubbing it into the flesh. Arrange the salmon in the grill basket and top it with a single layer of onion slices and the slices of 1 lemon. If using dried dill and fennel seeds, scatter them over the onion and lemon. Close the basket.

Lay the fennel stalks or fresh dill, if using, on the grill rack, then position the grill basket on top of them. Cover the grill with the hood and grill the salmon, with the vent open, for 20 to 30 minutes, or until an instant-reading meat thermometer placed in the thickest portion of the salmon registers 115 degrees.

Using 2 metal spatulas, transfer the salmon to a cutting board or platter, sprinkle with salt and pepper to taste, and garnish with the remaining lemon slices.

MENU

SALMON BARBECUED WITH FENNEL, LEMON, AND ONION

WILD RICE WITH GOLDEN RAISINS

MINTED CUCUMBER SALAD
(PAGE 122)

ORANGE SHERBET WITH SUGARED MINT LEAVES

ESPRESSO

GRILLED SOLE FILLETS WITH SHALLOT-GINGER GLAZE

4 SOLE FILLETS OR OTHER FIRM-FLESHED WHITE FISH (ABOUT 1½ POUNDS TOTAL)

6 SHALLOTS OR 1 MEDIUM ONION, COARSELY CHOPPED

4 QUARTER-SIZE SLICES, CUT ¼ INCH THICK, FRESH GINGER, UNPEELED

1 CLOVE GARLIC

3 TABLESPOONS UNSALTED BUTTER

½ CUP CHICKEN BROTH

4 TEASPOONS CORNSTARCH

⅓ CUP DRY WHITE WINE

1 TABLESPOON FRESH LEMON JUICE

2 TEASPOONS GRATED LEMON ZEST

¼ TEASPOON FRESHLY GROUND BLACK PEPPER

Preheat the grill. Spray a grilling basket with nonstick cooking spray and arrange the sole fillets in the basket.

In a food processor, mince the shallots, ginger, and garlic.

In a small skillet, warm the butter over medium-high heat until melted. Add the shallot-ginger mixture and cook, stirring, until the mixture is just golden, 8 to 10 minutes. Remove the skillet from the heat.

Brush the sole fillets with half of the shallot-ginger mixture and close the basket. Grill the fillets 4 to 5 inches from the heat, turning them once, until lightly colored and the flesh just flakes when tested with a fork, about 6 minutes.

Meanwhile, in a small bowl, blend together the chicken broth and cornstarch.

Return the skillet to medium heat and stir in the wine, lemon juice, lemon zest, and pepper. Bring to a boil, add the cornstarch mixture, and bring to a boil, stirring constantly. Reduce the heat to medium-low and simmer, stirring occasionally, for 1 minute, or until thickened and slightly glossy.

Arrange the sole fillets on a heated platter and drizzle the shallot-ginger glaze over them. Serve immediately.

GRILLED SOLE FILLETS WITH SHALLOT-GINGER GLAZE

GRILLED SWORDFISH WITH SPICY TROPICAL SAUCE

SERVES 4

1 ORANGE, PEELED AND COARSELY
CHOPPED

1 SMALL RED ONION, COARSELY CHOPPED

2 TABLESPOONS CHOPPED
SCALLION GREENS

1 CAN (8 OUNCES) CRUSHED PINEAPPLE,
PACKED IN JUICE

3 TABLESPOONS TOMATO PASTE

3 CLOVES GARLIC, MINCED OR CRUSHED
THROUGH A PRESS

2 TEASPOONS CORNSTARCH

¾ TEASPOON SUGAR

½ TEASPOON SALT

¼ TEASPOON RED PEPPER FLAKES

PINCH OF GROUND RED PEPPER

1 TABLESPOON OLIVE OIL

2 LARGE SWORDFISH STEAKS, EACH CUT
1 INCH THICK (ABOUT 1½ POUNDS
TOTAL), HALVED TO MAKE 4 EQUAL
PIECES

GRILLED SWORDFISH WITH SPICY TROPICAL SAUCE

Preheat the grill. Spray the grill with nonstick cooking spray.

In a medium saucepan, combine the orange, onion, scallion greens, pineapple and its juice, tomato paste, garlic, cornstarch, sugar, salt, red pepper flakes, and red pepper. Bring to a boil over medium heat, stirring frequently, and cook, uncovered, stirring occasionally, for 10 minutes. Reduce the heat to low and simmer, uncovered, until thickened, about 10 minutes. Keep the sauce warm over low heat.

Brush the swordfish with the olive oil. Season with salt and ground red pepper to taste. Grill the swordfish steaks 4 inches from the heat for about 6 minutes on each side, or until lightly colored and the flesh just flakes when tested with a fork. Transfer the fish to a heated platter and immediately pour the warm tropical sauce over it.

MENU

GRILLED SHIITAKE MUSHROOMS

GRILLED SWORDFISH WITH
SPICY TROPICAL SAUCE

WILD RICE PILAF

WATERCRESS AND HAZELNUT SALAD
(PAGE 103)

STRAWBERRY SHORTCAKE

GRILLED GROUPER WITH ROASTED PEPPER MEDLEY

1¼ POUNDS GROUPER FILLETS, SKIN LEFT ON, CUT INTO 4 PIECES

1½ TABLESPOONS EXTRA-VIRGIN OLIVE OIL, PLUS ADDITIONAL FOR DRIZZLING

2 LIMES, 1 JUICED, THE OTHER CUT INTO WEDGES

½ TEASPOON SALT

FRESHLY GROUND BLACK PEPPER

1 LARGE RED BELL PEPPER

1 LARGE ORANGE BELL PEPPER

1 LARGE GREEN BELL PEPPER

1 TABLESPOON CHOPPED FRESH TARRAGON, OR MORE TO TASTE

Preheat the grill. Spray a grill basket with nonstick cooking spray.

Put the grouper, skin-side down, in a shallow, nonreactive dish. In a small bowl, combine the olive oil, lime juice, salt, and black pepper to taste. Brush the marinade on the exposed side of the grouper.

Let the fish marinate, covered, for 30 minutes.

Meanwhile, grill the bell peppers about 4 to 5 inches from the heat, turning them frequently, until their skins blacken, about 10 to 15 minutes. Remove the peppers from the grill and transfer them to a brown paper bag. Close the bag tightly.

When the peppers are cool enough to handle, peel off their skins. Derib, seed, and slice the skinned peppers thinly and evenly. Divide the slices among 4 dinner plates, then drizzle them with olive oil to taste. Sprinkle the fresh tarragon on top.

Place the grouper in the grill basket and grill it, skin-side down, for 10 to 15 minutes. Turn the fish and grill for 5 minutes more.

Top each serving of bell peppers with a piece of grouper and garnish with a lime wedge. Serve immediately.

GRILLED SHRIMP IN THE SHELL WITH HERBED MUSTARD BUTTER

1 STICK (½ CUP) BUTTER, CUT INTO PIECES

2 CLOVES GARLIC, MINCED

½ CUP BEER

2 TABLESPOONS WHOLE-GRAIN SHARP MUSTARD, PREFERABLY CREOLE

1½ TO 2 POUNDS LARGE UNSHELLED SHRIMP

¼ CUP CHOPPED FRESH ROSEMARY OR 1 TABLESPOON DRIED

1 TEASPOON BLACK PEPPERCORNS, CRUSHED

1 BAY LEAF

¼ TEASPOON SALT

PARSLEY SPRIGS, FOR GARNISH

Preheat the grill. Spray a grill basket with nonstick cooking spray.

In a small saucepan, melt the butter with the garlic over low heat, being careful that the garlic does not brown.

In a glass bowl, whisk together the beer and mustard. Whisking constantly, drizzle in the garlic butter until thoroughly incorporated. Add the shrimp, rosemary, peppercorns, bay leaf, and salt, and, with a wooden spoon, stir to coat the shrimp.

With a slotted spoon, remove the shrimp from the sauce and arrange them in one layer in the grill basket; close the basket. Keep the sauce warm.

Grill the shrimp about 4 inches from the heat until they turn orange, 2 to 3 minutes per side. Return the grilled shrimp to the bowl, and toss to coat them with the reserved sauce. Serve immediately, garnished with the parsley sprigs.

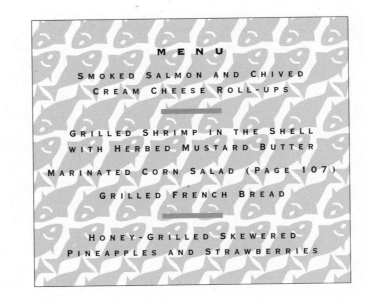

MENU

SMOKED SALMON AND CHIVED CREAM CHEESE ROLL-UPS

GRILLED SHRIMP IN THE SHELL WITH HERBED MUSTARD BUTTER

MARINATED CORN SALAD (PAGE 107)

GRILLED FRENCH BREAD

HONEY-GRILLED SKEWERED PINEAPPLES AND STRAWBERRIES

2 TABLESPOONS TAMARI OR OTHER
SOY SAUCE

½ TEASPOON GROUND CUMIN

1 CUP MINCED PARSLEY

½ CUP FRESH LIME JUICE

1 CUP OLIVE OIL

2-INCH PIECE FRESH GINGER, CUT INTO
⅛-INCH-THICK SLICES

FOUR 8-OUNCE MAKO SHARK, OR
BLUEFIN OR ALBACORE TUNA

1⅓ CUPS SOUR CREAM

1 LIME, THINLY SLICED, FOR GARNISH

GRILLED MAKO SHARK WITH PARSLIED SOUR CREAM SAUCE

Preheat the grill.

In a small bowl, combine the tamari, cumin, parsley, lime juice, olive oil, and ginger and stir well to combine; set aside.

Brush the steaks on both sides with the oil that has risen to the top of reserved basting sauce. Grill the steaks 4 to 5 inches from the heat, turning them once, for 8 to 10 minutes, or until the flesh just flakes when tested with a fork.

Transfer the steaks to a heated platter and cover loosely with aluminum foil to keep them warm.

Meanwhile, with a small slotted spoon, remove the ginger from the marinade and discard; purée the sauce in a food processor or blender. In a small saucepan, bring the sauce to a simmer over medium heat, stirring occasionally, for 2 to 3 minutes.

Place the sour cream in a medium bowl and gradually add the warmed sauce, stirring until completely incorporated.

Divide the steaks among 4 heated dinner plates and top each with a generous dollop of the parslied sour cream sauce. Garnish the sauce on each serving with a slice of lime and serve at once. Serve the remaining sauce on the side

THE FIXINGS

THE FIXINGS

Cooking outdoors lends itself to simple, relaxed preparations—warm-weather foods, if you will—and what better way to prepare them than to use the preheated grill for cooking the accompaniments as well? Add a rice or pasta salad, frequently best made in advance to allow the flavor of the dressing to marry with the ingredients, and a dessert, and the meal is not only complete, but the doing of it has remained remarkably easy, too. Side dishes during the summer months include the obvious—vegetables, fresh from either your garden or your favorite farm stand—and they make superb light accompaniments to grilled fish or shellfish.

VEGETABLES ON THE GRILL

Every vegetable—large or small, tender or tough, whole or sliced—is potentially a candidate for either grilling on a rack, roasting in embers, or steaming in a wrapper. Which method to adopt depends on the nature of the vegetable and the effect desired by the cook. Generally speaking, whole vegetables can be either roasted or grilled. Sliced vegetables are best grilled (in a grilling basket or on skewers) or steamed—although they can also be roasted if well wrapped in aluminum foil.

WHOLE VEGETABLES: WHEN TO GRILL . . . AND WHEN TO ROAST

Almost every vegetable with a protective skin or firm outer flesh—and there are many of them, when you stop to think about it—lends itself to being grilled or roasted whole. All the cook need do is turn the vegetables from time to time, making either grilling or roasting whole vegetables a relatively fret-free way to prepare a delicious side dish for grilled foods.

Among those large whole vegetables that can be simply placed on a grilling rack suspended over properly preheated embers are new potatoes, baking potatoes, sweet potatoes or yams, mature boiling potatoes, zucchini, pattypan and yellow squashes, cucumbers, eggplants, sweet bell peppers, and scallions. When grilling whole vegetables on a rack, they should cook 4 to 6 inches above a fire that has burned down until it is still hot but not scorching. Periodic turning will ensure that they cook through at an even rate. Grilled whole vegetables become tender and develop a subtly smoky taste when treated this way.

To keep the skins of grilled whole vegetables tender, oil them liberally before cooking. This is also an good opportunity to add more flavor to the vegetables by using flavored oils. The vegetables must also be pierced or scored to keep the skins from bursting when their juices expand as steam. Long vegetables, such as squashes, cucumbers, and eggplant, should be scored with long, deep grooves; rounder vegetables, such as potatoes, should simply be pricked. Small whole vegetables (new potatoes, baby beets) can be threaded onto skewers.

Thicker-skinned vegetables—onions, winter squashes, garlic bulbs, and beets, for example—can be cooked directly in the live coals of the fire. In most cases, they should first be wrapped in foil to prevent their juices from escaping. Baking potatoes and sweet potatoes or yams can be either roasted or grilled. As with grilling, whole vegetables should be pricked first before roasting so they will not explode.

SLICED IS NICE

Vegetables cut into slices, chunks, or segments acquire an appetizing brown finish and wonderful deep flavor when grilled. And they cook quickly, another boon to the busy chef. Because their cut surfaces are exposed to direct heat, vegetable pieces should first be coated with oil to keep them moist. Think of this as an opportunity to suffuse the vegetables with extra flavor: Brush them with a fragrant dark sesame, hazelnut, or basil-infused oil, or add your own herbs and other seasonings to a fine olive oil.

The best vegetables to grill in slices are those with firm, moist flesh—among them, eggplants, summer squashes, sweet bell peppers, onions, and underripe or green tomatoes. Root vegetables, such as white potatoes, sweet potatoes, and turnips, and fibrous fennel or celery ribs are also suitable, but they must be parboiled in advance until about half-cooked so they do not char outside before becoming tender within.

The size of the slices will determine whether you grill them directly on the grill rack, thread them onto skewers for kebabs, or arrange them in a hinged grilling basket. Pieces large enough for easy turning with tongs or a spatula can go individually onto the grill rack in a single layer. If the pieces are small or fragile—or if there are so many pieces that turning them one at a time would be difficult to complete in a timely fashion—either form kebabs with them or use a grilling basket brushed or sprayed first with nonstick cooking spray.

For grilling on a rack or in a basket, vegetables, such as squash or onions, should ideally be cut into slices about a third of an inch thick, although any particularly juicy ones might be cut into half-inch-thick pieces. In either case, be sure that all of the slices are the same thickness so that they will be done simultaneously. And don't forget to oil them all generously before cooking. A sprig or two of fresh herbs added to the basket before grilling will also enhance the aromatic outcome.

For skewering, the slices can be somewhat thinner or thicker, but they should be similar in diameter—1½ to 2 inches. If you intend to grill vegetables of two radically different densities—cherry tomatoes and beets, for example—you can either keep all the vegetables of like density together on one skewer, or you can parboil the harder vegetable for a minute or two so it will cook at the same speed as the softer vegetable.

When assembling a kebab—or a brochette, as it is often called— begin and end the skewer with a firm-fleshed vegetable, such as a piece of red bell pepper, which will serve as an anchor for juicier pieces, such as zucchini. That said, the more colorful the variety of vegetables you alternate on the skewers, the prettier the accompaniment, the prettier the plate.

WRAPPING WILL SEAL IN JUICES

When vegetables are enclosed in wrappers before grilling or roasting, they can be cooked by steam heat. This method also allows for the addition of ingredients that can cook along with the vegetables to form a simple sauce. Furthermore, wrappers keep the contents hot for 10 minutes, or even longer, thus simplifying the timing of an outdoor meal.

Only corn on the cob comes with its own natural wrapping—its husk. The husks must first be pulled back so that all the silk can be removed, then reassembled and tied at the end with a piece of kitchen twine. Soaking the reassembled ears in water ensures that there will be enough liquid to create steam.

For other vegetables, heavy-duty aluminum foil can be shaped into sturdy packets. Wrapped in this manner, any vegetable—tough carrots or cabbage as well as tender squashes and mushrooms—can be easily steamed. A double layer of foil is essential to make the packets sturdy, and the edges should be double-folded to guarantee airtightness, a prerequisite for steaming. And although the sizes of the packets can vary from individual servings to plattersful, it is best to keep them light enough to be handled with ease.

Prepare vegetables for grilling in wrappers as you would those for eating: Peel, core, shell, or stem according to the type, then slice, cut up, or divide into sections as desired. Whole potatoes in the jackets should be pierced or scored around the middle to prevent them from bursting.

If a single vegetable is packeted, cut all the pieces in similar size so that they steam at the same rate. When cooked in combination, tougher vegetables should be cut into smaller pieces than tender kinds and the tougher ones placed at the bottom of the packet, where the temperature will be highest.

Juicy vegetables—squashes and the like—by nature supply all the moisture required for steaming; less moist vegetables should be dipped in water before wrapping. A chunk of butter will provide enrichment, and adding a few drops of stock, citrus juice, vinegar, or wine will also supply flavor as well as moisture. As you will see when you open up the packets for serving, it is the flavor of the steamed vegetables themselves that bursts forth. If you are of a mind to embellish those, consider adding to the wrappers a dusting of grated cheese, bits of lightly sautéed bacon, or fresh or dried herbs.

VEGETABLE, NECTARINE, AND FETA KEBABS WITH MINT-YOGURT SAUCE

¼ POUND EGGPLANT, CUT INTO EIGHT 1-INCH CUBES

¼ TEASPOON SALT

8 SMALL NEW POTATOES (ABOUT ¾ POUND)

2 ONIONS, QUARTERED

2 RED OR ORANGE BELL PEPPERS, SEEDED, DERIBBED, AND EACH CUT INTO 8 SQUARES

1 SMALL UNPEELED CUCUMBER, CUT INTO 8 THICK SLICES

8 LARGE MUSHROOMS

2 NECTARINES, QUARTERED

7 OUNCES FETA CHEESE, CUT INTO 8 CUBES

2 TABLESPOONS EXTRA-VIRGIN OLIVE OIL

1¼ CUPS PLAIN LOWFAT YOGURT

3 TABLESPOONS CHOPPED FRESH MINT

1 CLOVE GARLIC, CRUSHED (OPTIONAL)

FRESH GRAPES LEAVES, FOR SERVING (OPTIONAL)

Preheat the grill. Spray the grill with nonstick cooking spray.

In a colander, sprinkle the eggplant cubes with the salt; set aside to drain for 30 minutes.

Meanwhile, cook the potatoes and onions in a pan of simmering water for 15 to 20 minutes, until just tender. Drain and let cool.

Put the eggplant in a large saucepan of boiling water. Return the water to a boil, reduce the heat, and simmer for 2 minutes. Add the peppers and cook for 1 minute; add the cucumber and cook for 1 minute. Drain the vegetables and let cool.

Sprinkle the cooked vegetables, mushrooms, nectarines, and cheese with the olive oil. Starting and ending with a piece of bell pepper, thread the vegetables, nectarine pieces, and cheese onto eight 10-inch metal skewers to make kebabs.

Grill the kebabs 4 to 5 inches from the heat, turning them frequently, until tender and lightly charred, about 15 minutes.

While the kebabs grill, in a serving bowl, combine the yogurt, mint, and garlic, if using.

Transfer the kebabs to a platter covered with grape leaves, if desired, and serve with the mint sauce.

4 MEDIUM IDAHO POTATOES

4 TABLESPOONS UNSALTED BUTTER,
AT ROOM TEMPERATURE

¼ TEASPOON PAPRIKA

¼ TEASPOON DRIED OREGANO

¼ TEASPOON DRIED BASIL

¼ TEASPOON SALT

PINCH OF FRESHLY GROUND
BLACK PEPPER

ROASTED HERBED POTATO FANS

Preheat the grill. Cut four 8-inch-square pieces of aluminum foil.

Scrub the potatoes, rinse, and pat them dry with paper towels. Cut the potatoes crosswise into ¼-inch-thick slices without cutting all the way through the flesh. The slices should remain attached. Place each potato in the center of a square of aluminum foil, fold the edges together, and crimp to seal airtight.

Place the packets directly in the hot coals and cook, turning them several times, for about 40 minutes.

Meanwhile, cream the butter, then beat in the paprika, oregano, basil, salt, and pepper until blended and smooth.

With tongs, transfer the packets to a heated platter. Unwrap each, and with a pastry brush, spread each potato with some of the herbed butter, coating the inside surfaces of each slice. Rewrap the packets loosely and return the potatoes to the coals. Cook for 10 to 15 minutes more, or until the flesh yields easily when tested with the tines of a fork. To serve, unwrap the packets and serve at once, spread into fans.

SERVES 4

2 YELLOW BELL PEPPERS

2 GREEN BELL PEPPERS

¼ CUP OLIVE OIL

6 CLOVES GARLIC, MINCED

SALT AND FRESHLY GROUND
BLACK PEPPER

GRILLED YELLOW AND GREEN BELL PEPPERS

Preheat the grill.

Arrange the peppers around the edge of the grill, 4 inches from the heat. Grill, turning them often with tongs to make sure they char evenly, for 20 to 30 minutes, or until blackened all over. The yellow peppers will take about 5 minutes longer to grill than green peppers.

Transfer the peppers to a paper bag, and close it tightly. Let the peppers steam in the bag until cool enough to handle, about 10 minutes. Peel the charred skin from the peppers, then core, quarter, and seed the peppers.

In a small bowl, combine the oil and garlic.

Arrange the quartered peppers on a platter, alternating yellow and green pieces. Spoon the garlic oil over them, and season generously with salt and pepper to taste.

½ CUP OLIVE OIL

2 CLOVES GARLIC, MINCED

2 TEASPOONS CHOPPED FRESH OREGANO
OR 1 TEASPOON DRIED

2 TEASPOONS CHOPPED FRESH BASIL OR
1 TEASPOON DRIED

1 TEASPOON SALT

½ TEASPOON FRESHLY GROUND
BLACK PEPPER

2 MEDIUM YELLOW SQUASH, CUT INTO
1-INCH PIECES

2 MEDIUM GREEN BELL PEPPERS,
SEEDED, DERIBBED, AND CUT INTO
1-INCH SQUARES

16 CHERRY TOMATOES

16 MEDIUM MUSHROOMS

GRILLED VEGETABLE KEBABS

Preheat the grill.

In a small bowl, stir together the oil, garlic, oregano, basil, salt, and pepper.

Alternating the vegetables, thread them onto eight 10-inch metal skewers, beginning and ending each skewer with a mushroom. Brush the skewered vegetables with the olive oil mixture.

Grill the kebabs 4 inches from the heat, turning and basting them frequently, for about 5 minutes per side, or until the vegetables are tender.

4 EARS CORN, UNHUSKED

4 TABLESPOONS UNSALTED BUTTER,
AT ROOM TEMPERATURE

1 TEASPOON CHOPPED FRESH BASIL
OR ½ TEASPOON DRIED

1 TEASPOON CHOPPED FRESH OREGANO
OR ½ TEASPOON DRIED

¼ TEASPOON SALT

¼ TEASPOON FRESHLY GROUND
BLACK PEPPER

ROASTED HERBED CORN ON THE COB

Preheat the grill. Cut 4 large squares of aluminum foil for wrapping each ear of corn.

Peel back but do not remove the corn husks on each ear. Remove and discard the corn silk.

In a small bowl, blend together the butter, basil, oregano, salt, and pepper.

Spread about 1 tablespoon of herbed butter over each ear of corn, then close the husk around the corn.

Wrap each ear of corn tightly in a square of aluminum foil. Place the wrapped ears in the coals and roast them, turning them occasionally, for 30 minutes, or until tender. Serve at once.

ROASTED HERBED CORN ON THE COB

SWEET POTATO AND APPLE SALAD WITH LIME-YOGURT DRESSING

6 SMALL SWEET POTATOES (ABOUT 1½ POUNDS TOTAL)

⅓ CUP PLAIN LOWFAT YOGURT

3 TABLESPOONS MAYONNAISE

1 TABLESPOON FRESH LIME JUICE

¾ TEASPOON GRATED LIME ZEST

1 TEASPOON LIGHT BROWN SUGAR

¼ TEASPOON SALT

¼ TEASPOON GROUND PEPPER, PREFERABLY WHITE

1 LARGE GRANNY SMITH APPLE, UNPEELED

2 RIBS CELERY, COARSELY CHOPPED

⅓ CUP WALNUTS, LIGHTLY TOASTED, IF DESIRED, AND COARSELY CHOPPED

SWEET POTATO AND APPLE SALAD WITH LIME-YOGURT DRESSING

Preheat the grill (or the oven to 400 degrees). If using the grill, cut 1 or 2 slits in each potato as steam vents, then wrap each in aluminum foil. Place the potatoes directly in the coals and roast, turning them several times, for 30 minutes, or until the flesh is tender when tested with the tines of a fork. Remove and unwrap to cool partially.

If using the oven, line a baking sheet with foil. Cut 1 or 2 slits in the sweet potatoes as steam vents. Place the potatoes on the baking sheet and bake for 30 minutes, until tender.

Meanwhile, in a large serving bowl, combine the yogurt, mayonnaise, lime juice, lime zest, brown sugar, salt, and pepper.

Coarsely chop the apple, add it to the dressing, and toss. Add the celery and walnuts and stir to combine.

When the potatoes are cool enough to handle but still warm, peel them and cut them into bite-size pieces. Add the still-warm potatoes to the serving bowl and toss to coat with the dressing. Serve the salad at room temperature.

8 SMALL LEEKS

4 MEDIUM ZUCCHINI, EACH ABOUT
6 INCHES LONG, ENDS REMOVED

8 MEDIUM TOMATOES

¼ CUP CHOPPED FRESH BASIL OR
2 TABLESPOONS DRIED

½ CUP SWEET APPLE CIDER

SALT AND FRESHLY GROUND
BLACK PEPPER

MELANGE OF FRESH VEGETABLES EN PAPILLOTE

Preheat the grill. Cut four 12-inch squares of aluminum foil.

With a sharp knife, trim off and discard the tough green tops and roots from the leeks. Split the leeks lengthwise and rinse thoroughly under cold running water to remove all sand and grit.

With the knife, quarter each zucchini lengthwise.

Plunge the tomatoes into a saucepan of boiling water and blanch them for 30 seconds. With a slotted spoon, transfer them to a colander and refresh under cold running water. Peel and seed the tomatoes, then quarter them.

Divide the chopped vegetables evenly among the aluminum squares and sprinkle each portion with basil and 2 tablespoons of the cider. Fold the edges of the foil together and crimp to seal airtight.

Place the packets on the grill and cook for 15 minutes. To serve, unwrap the packets and season the vegetables with salt and pepper to taste.

3 SMALL RED BELL PEPPERS (ABOUT
¾ POUND TOTAL)

¼ POUND SNOW PEAS, STRINGS
REMOVED, OR TINY GREEN BEANS

1 TABLESPOON DIJON MUSTARD

½ TEASPOON CREOLE MUSTARD

2 SCALLIONS, FINELY CHOPPED

2 TABLESPOONS TARRAGON VINEGAR OR
WHITE WINE VINEGAR

¼ CUP MINCED FRESH TARRAGON OR
OREGANO, LOOSELY PACKED, OR
1 TEASPOON DRIED

½ CUP EXTRA-VIRGIN OLIVE OIL

SALT AND FRESHLY GROUND
BLACK PEPPER

1 SMALL HEAD OF BOSTON LETTUCE,
SEPARATED INTO LEAVES

2 TOMATOES (ABOUT 1 POUND),
CUT INTO SLICES ½ INCH THICK

ROASTED RED PEPPER, SNOW PEA, AND TOMATO SALAD

Preheat the grill.

Place the peppers on the grill rack and roast them, turning them until the skins are blackened all over, about 10 minutes in all. With tongs, remove the charred peppers to a paper bag, close it tightly, and let the peppers steam until cool enough to handle, about 15 minutes.

In a saucepan, blanch the snow peas or green beans in boiling water for 2 minutes. Drain in colander and refresh under cold running water; pat dry with paper towels.

In a bowl, combine the mustards, scallions, vinegar, and tarragon or oregano, whisking until smooth. Gradually drizzle in the oil, whisking constantly, until the dressing is thick and smooth and the consistency of mayonnaise. Add salt and pepper to taste.

Remove the peppers from the bag and peel off the charred skins. Halve, seed, and derib the peppers. Cut into ½-inch-wide strips.

Line a platter with the lettuce leaves and arrange the tomatoes, snow peas, and roasted pepper strips decoratively on top. Pour the dressing over the salad.

MIXED VEGETABLES WITH SUN-DRIED TOMATO AND SHALLOT MARINADE

1 SMALL EGGPLANT, CUT INTO ¾-INCH-THICK SLICES

1 TABLESPOON PLUS ¼ TEASPOON SALT

1 TABLESPOON PLUS ¼ CUP FRESH LEMON JUICE

6 OUNCES SMALL YOUNG OKRA

1 SMALL FENNEL BULB, CUT INTO 6 WEDGES, TOP RESERVED AND CHOPPED

1 MEDIUM ZUCCHINI, SLICED DIAGONALLY INTO ¾-INCH PIECES

1 RED BELL PEPPER, CUT INTO 12 STRIPS

1 ORANGE BELL PEPPER, CUT INTO 12 STRIPS

2 TABLESPOONS EXTRA-VIRGIN OLIVE OIL

12 SMALL SHALLOTS

1 CLOVE GARLIC

6 OIL-PACKED SUN-DRIED TOMATOES, QUARTERED

1½ TEASPOONS CHOPPED PARSLEY

1½ TEASPOONS CHOPPED FRESH THYME

1½ TEASPOONS CHOPPED FRESH OREGANO

2 PITTED BLACK OLIVES, SLICED INTO THIN RINGS

FRESHLY GROUND BLACK PEPPER

In a colander, sprinkle the eggplant with 1 tablespoon of the salt; set aside to drain for 30 minutes. Rinse well and pat dry.

Add the 1 tablespoon lemon juice to a nonreactive pan of boiling water. Blanch the okra for 5 seconds; add the fennel and blanch for 10 seconds. Drain the vegetables, refresh under cold running water, and drain again. Let cool, halve the okra lengthwise.

Combine the eggplant, okra, fennel, zucchini, and pepper strips in a large bowl.

In a nonreactive skillet over low heat, heat the olive oil until hot but not smoking and add the shallots. Cook, turning them, until golden brown, about 8 minutes. Add the garlic and cook for 20 seconds.

Remove the pan from the heat and stir in the sun-dried tomato quarters; let the mixture infuse and cool for about 15 minutes. Add the ¼ cup lemon juice, parsley, thyme, oregano, olives, ¼ teaspoon salt, and some black pepper. Stir in the reserved fennel top.

Pour the marinade over the vegetables and toss gently. Cover the bowl and marinate at room temperature, turning occasionally, for at least 1 hour, or overnight in the refrigerator.

Preheat the grill. Cut 6 rectangles of aluminum foil, each measuring about 24 by 12 inches, and fold them in half crosswise. Pile one-sixth of the marinated vegetable mixture in the center of a foil square. Bring the top and bottom edges of the square together, fold them over twice to seal, then fold in the sides of the square, to make a packet. Make 5 more packets in the same way.

Grill the packets 4 to 5 inches from the heat for 20 to 30 minutes. Transfer the packets to a platter and unwrap them partially to serve.

HERBED NEW POTATOES, CARROTS, AND SCALLIONS

16 SMALL NEW POTATOES (ABOUT 2 POUNDS TOTAL)

12 BABY FINGER CARROTS (ABOUT ½ POUND TOTAL), PEELED

9 SCALLIONS, TRIMMED, LEAVING 2 INCHES OF GREEN, OR 18 PEARL ONIONS, PEELED

½ CUP EXTRA-VIRGIN OLIVE OIL

1 TABLESPOON MINCED FRESH SAGE, ROSEMARY, OR THYME OR 1 TEASPOON DRIED

SALT AND FRESHLY GROUND BLACK PEPPER

Preheat the grill.

In a large bowl, combine the potatoes, carrots, and scallions, and drizzle the olive oil over all; toss until evenly coated. Sprinkle the vegetables with sage, rosemary, or thyme and toss again.

Cut four 12-inch squares of aluminum foil and divide the potatoes and carrots evenly among them. With a slotted spoon, transfer the potatoes and carrots to the lower half of each piece of foil and arrange them in a single layer. Fold down the top half of square, being careful not to disturb vegetables, and crimp the edges to seal. Reserve the oil remaining in the bowl.

Place the packets on the grill about 4 to 5 inches from the heat and cook for 15 minutes.

With tongs or a metal spatula, carefully remove the packets from the grill. Open the packets and add the scallions or onions next to, not on top of, the potatoes and carrots. Drizzle the remaining herbed oil over them. Reseal the packets and place on grill, turning them so that the "uncooked" side is down. Grill for 15 minutes. Remove the packets from the grill and leave sealed until ready to serve.

To serve, open the packets and turn the vegetables into a heated serving bowl; season with salt and several generous grindings of pepper.

MACARONI AND BELL PEPPER SALAD WITH CILANTRO MAYONNAISE

2 CUPS ELBOW MACARONI (ABOUT 9 OUNCES)

1 TEASPOON VEGETABLE OIL

1 CUP MAYONNAISE

¼ CUP CIDER VINEGAR

3 TABLESPOONS DIJON MUSTARD

⅓ CUP CHOPPED CILANTRO

1 ½ TEASPOONS CELERY SEEDS, CRUSHED

½ TEASPOON SALT

½ TEASPOON FRESHLY GROUND BLACK PEPPER

⅛ TEASPOON GROUND RED PEPPER

1 CUP DICED GREEN BELL PEPPER

1 CUP DICED CARROTS

1 CUP CHOPPED PITTED SMALL BLACK OLIVES

In a large saucepan of boiling salted water, cook the macaroni according to package directions, until tender but still firm. Drain, rinse under cold running water, and drain again. Return the macaroni to the pan and toss it with the oil; set aside.

In a large bowl, combine the mayonnaise, vinegar, mustard, cilantro, celery seeds, salt, black pepper, and red pepper, and stir until well blended.

Add the macaroni, bell pepper, carrots, and olives to the dressing, and toss gently until the macaroni is well coated. Cover the bowl and refrigerate the salad for at least 1 hour, or until the flavors are blended.

GREEN AND WHITE RICE SALAD WITH TARRAGON-WALNUT VINAIGRETTE

1½ CUPS LONG-GRAIN RICE

1½ CUPS SHELLED FRESH PEAS OR FROZEN PEAS, THAWED

½ CUCUMBER, CUT INTO ¼-INCH DICE

½ SMALL ZUCCHINI, JULIENNED

3 SCALLIONS, THINLY SLICED DIAGONALLY

1 TABLESPOON MINCED FRESH CHIVES

3 TABLESPOONS CHOPPED PARSLEY

½ TEASPOON DIJON MUSTARD

⅛ TEASPOON SALT

FRESHLY GROUND BLACK PEPPER

2 TABLESPOONS TARRAGON VINEGAR

¼ CUP WALNUT OR EXTRA-VIRGIN OLIVE OIL

1 HEAD OF BIBB LETTUCE, LEAVES SEPARATED

Cook the rice in a large saucepan of simmering salted water until just tender, 15 to 20 minutes. Drain the rice in a colander, rinse it under cold running water, and let it drain. Set the rice aside to cool.

Blanch the fresh peas in boiling water for about 30 seconds; if you are using frozen peas, add them to boiling water and just bring the water back to a boil. Drain the peas, refresh them under cold running water, and drain them again.

Transfer the cooled rice to a large bowl, add the peas, cucumber, and zucchini, and combine the vegetables well. Stir in the scallions, chives, and parsley.

In a bowl, whisk together the mustard, salt, pepper to taste, and vinegar. Add the oil, whisking until well blended.

Pour the dressing over the salad, and toss it thoroughly. Cover and let the salad stand at room temperature for 30 minutes to blend the flavors.

To serve, line a large serving bowl with the lettuce leaves and pile the salad in the center.

SERVES 6

SHREDDED CARROT SALAD WITH PECANS AND RED ONION

6 MEDIUM CARROTS (ABOUT 1 POUND), PEELED

1 SMALL RED ONION

¾ CUP MAYONNAISE

4 TABLESPOONS FRESH LEMON JUICE

2 TEASPOONS GRATED LEMON ZEST

1 TABLESPOON DIJON MUSTARD

1 TEASPOON DRY MUSTARD

¼ TEASPOON FRESHLY GROUND BLACK PEPPER

¼ TEASPOON SUGAR

1 CUP CHOPPED PECANS

1 CUP GOLDEN RAISINS

In a food processor, shred the carrots.

By hand, halve the onion lengthwise, then cut it crosswise into thin half-rings.

In a large serving bowl, combine the mayonnaise, lemon juice, lemon zest, Dijon and dry mustards, the pepper, and sugar.

Add the carrots, onion, pecans, and raisins, and toss to combine.

SERVES 6

BROCCOLI SALAD WITH RED ONION AND YELLOW PEPPER

3 STALKS BROCCOLI

2 CLOVES GARLIC, UNPEELED

1 LARGE YELLOW BELL PEPPER

1 SMALL RED ONION

¼ CUP OLIVE OR OTHER VEGETABLE OIL

2 TABLESPOONS RED WINE VINEGAR

1 ½ TEASPOONS DRY MUSTARD

½ TEASPOON SALT

3 TABLESPOONS FRESHLY GROUND BLACK PEPPER

3 TABLESPOONS CHOPPED CHIVES OR SCALLION GREENS (OPTIONAL)

Cut the tops off the broccoli stalks. Cut the stalks into bite-size pieces and separate the tops into florets.

Steam the broccoli and the garlic in a steamer until the broccoli is tender, 5 to 8 minutes.

Meanwhile, cut the bell pepper into thin strips. Cut the onion into thin slices.

Remove the garlic cloves from the steamer and set aside. Cool the broccoli by refreshing it under cold running water; drain well.

In a small bowl, whisk together the oil, vinegar, mustard, salt, black pepper, and chives (if using). Peel the cooked garlic and mash it with a fork; add it to the dressing, whisking well to blend.

Place the broccoli, bell pepper, onion and vinaigrette in a salad bowl and toss to combine.

CABBAGE, SNOW PEAS, AND CUCUMBER WITH CURRIED MAYONNAISE

SERVES 4

½ SMALL HEAD OF NAPPA OR CHINESE CABBAGE, TOUGH OUTER LEAVES REMOVED

¼ POUND SNOW PEAS, STRINGS REMOVED

1 SMALL CUCUMBER

⅓ TO ½ CUP MAYONNAISE

1 TABLESPOON VEGETABLE OIL

1 TABLESPOON WHITE WINE VINEGAR

1 TEASPOON CURRY POWDER

With a chef's knife, cut the cabbage crosswise into 1-inch wide pieces. In a colander, rinse the cabbage and drain.

With a chef's knife, cut the snow peas lengthwise into ¼-inch julienne strips. Add to the salad bowl.

Peel the cucumber, halve it lengthwise, and, with a teaspoon, scoop out the seeds. Cut each half crosswise into ½-inch-thick slices. Add to the salad bowl and toss to combine.

In a small bowl, whisk together the mayonnaise, oil, vinegar, and curry powder until well blended.

Spoon the dressing over the salad and toss to coat.

3 BUNCHES WATERCRESS OR
2 BUNCHES DANDELION GREENS
(ABOUT 1 POUND TOTAL)

1 CUP HAZELNUTS OR ½ CUP
SLIVERED ALMONDS

¼ CUP EXTRA-VIRGIN OLIVE OIL

JUICE OF 1 LARGE LEMON

SALT AND FRESHLY GROUND
BLACK PEPPER

WATERCRESS AND HAZELNUT SALAD

Preheat the oven to 350 degrees.

Remove and discard the tough stems from the watercress or trim off the dandelion stems. Place the greens in a salad bowl.

Spread the hazelnuts on a jelly-roll pan and toast them in the preheated oven for 4 to 6 minutes. (If using almonds, toast for 3 to 4 minutes, or until very lightly browned.) Rub the hazelnuts together in a kitchen towel to remove their skins. Then coarsely chop the nuts.

Spoon the olive oil over the watercress or dandelion greens and toss until evenly coated. Sprinkle on the lemon juice and toss again. Garnish the salad with the toasted nuts and season with salt and a generous grinding of pepper. Serve at once.

SERVES 6 TO 8

12 MEDIUM RED POTATOES (ABOUT 2 POUNDS)

¼ POUND BACON (4 TO 6 SLICES)

1 MEDIUM RED ONION, CHOPPED (ABOUT 1¼ CUPS)

3 TABLESPOONS FLOUR

1½ TABLESPOONS SUGAR

¾ TEASPOON DRY MUSTARD

¾ TEASPOON SALT

½ TEASPOON CELERY SEEDS

½ TEASPOON FRESHLY GROUND BLACK PEPPER

¾ CUP WATER

⅔ CUP CIDER VINEGAR

3 HARD-COOKED EGGS, COARSELY CHOPPED

1 SMALL GREEN BELL PEPPER, CHOPPED (ABOUT ¾ CUP)

1 CUP CHOPPED CELERY, INCLUDING THE LEAVES

¼ CUP CHOPPED PARSLEY

HOT GERMAN POTATO SALAD

In a large saucepan of simmering salted water, cook the potatoes until tender, 30 to 35 minutes. Drain and set aside.

Meanwhile, in a large nonreactive skillet, cook the bacon over medium heat until crisp, about 10 minutes. Reserving the fat, remove the bacon; crumble and set aside.

In the bacon fat, sauté the onion over medium heat until softened but not brown, about 10 minutes. Stir in the flour, sugar, mustard, salt, celery seeds, and black pepper. Reduce the heat to low and cook, stirring constantly, until the mixture has slightly thickened, about 5 minutes.

Remove the skillet from the heat and stir in the water and vinegar. Return the skillet to the heat and bring the dressing to a boil, stirring constantly. Cook, stirring, for 1 minute. Remove the skillet from the heat and stir the reserved crumbled bacon into the hot dressing.

Slice the unpeeled potatoes into the dressing and stir gently to coat them. Return the skillet to medium heat and cook, stirring gently, until the dressing is hot and bubbly, about 1 minute.

Transfer the hot potato salad to a large serving bowl. Stir in the eggs, green pepper, celery, and parsley. Serve the salad warm.

RATATOUILLE WITH MUSHROOMS

1½ POUNDS EGGPLANT, PEELED AND CUT INTO ¾-INCH PIECES

1½ TEASPOONS SALT

2 TABLESPOONS EXTRA-VIRGIN OLIVE OIL

2 LARGE ONIONS, CUT INTO THIN RINGS

4 CLOVES GARLIC, CRUSHED

¼ CUP DRY WHITE WINE

½ POUND LARGE CULTIVATED OR WILD MUSHROOMS, OR A COMBINATION OF BOTH, STEMMED AND SLICED

3 TABLESPOONS CHOPPED FRESH OREGANO OR 1 TABLESPOON DRIED

2 YELLOW BELL PEPPERS, BLANCHED AND CUT INTO 2½-INCH-LONG STRIPS

1 POUND PLUM TOMATOES (ABOUT 6), PEELED, SEEDED, AND COARSELY CHOPPED INTO ½-INCH PIECES

FRESHLY GROUND BLACK PEPPER

3 TABLESPOONS CHOPPED FRESH BASIL

In a bowl, toss the eggplant pieces with 1 teaspoon of the salt. Place the eggplant in a colander and weight it down with a plate small enough to rest on top of the pieces. Let the eggplant stand for 30 minutes.

Rinse the eggplant under cold running water and drain it well. Pat the pieces dry on paper towels.

In a large, nonreactive saucepan, heat the oil until hot but not smoking. Add the onions and cook them over low heat, stirring occasionally, until soft but not brown, about 8 minutes. Add the garlic and cook, stirring, for 1 minute.

Add the eggplant pieces, pour in the wine, and cook, uncovered, stirring, for 15 minutes. Stir in the mushrooms and oregano, cover the pan, and cook the mixture for 5 minutes.

Add the yellow peppers, the tomatoes, the remaining ½ teaspoon salt, and season generously with black pepper. Cook, stirring, until heated through, about 5 minutes. Remove the pan from the heat and stir in the basil. Transfer the ratatouille to a wide, shallow serving bowl and let it cool to room temperature.

1 POUND PASTA SHELLS

¼ POUND PECORINO ROMANO OR
PARMESAN CHEESE

2 CUPS FRESH BASIL LEAVES

2 CLOVES GARLIC, COARSELY CHOPPED

½ CUP PECAN HALVES

¾ CUP EXTRA-VIRGIN OLIVE OIL

SALT AND FRESHLY GROUND
BLACK PEPPER

PASTA SALAD
WITH PESTO

In a large saucepan, bring 2 quarts salted water to a boil over high heat. Add the pasta and cook, stirring occasionally, until al dente, 10 to 12 minutes, or according to package directions.

Meanwhile, in a food processor, grate enough cheese of choice to measure ½ cup. Add the basil leaves, garlic, and pecans and pulse until puréed. With the motor running, through the feed tube slowly pour in all but 2 tablespoons of the olive oil; process until combined. Season the pesto with salt and pepper to taste.

In a large colander, drain the pasta, return it to the pan, and toss with the remaining 2 tablespoons olive oil.

Pour the pesto over the warm shells and toss gently to combine. Transfer the pasta to a serving bowl and let cool.

MARINATED CORN SALAD

¼ CUP EXTRA-VIRGIN OLIVE OIL

6 LARGE SHALLOTS (ABOUT ¼ POUND TOTAL), CHOPPED

2 MEDIUM RED BELLPEPPERS, CUT INTO STRIPS

SALT AND FRESHLY GROUND BLACK PEPPER

4 EARS FRESH CORN OR TWO 10-OUNCE PACKAGES FROZEN KERNELS, THAWED

1 CLOVE GARLIC, MINCED

½ TEASPOON BLACK PEPPERCORNS, CRUSHED

1 TEASPOON CHOPPED FRESH THYME OR 1 TEASPOON DRIED

1½ TEASPOONS CHOPPED PARSLEY

3 TABLESPOONS DRY WHITE WINE

2 TEASPOONS SHERRY VINEGAR OR RED WINE VINEGAR

In a large skillet, heat 2 tablespoons of the olive oil over medium heat for 30 seconds. Reduce the heat to low, add the shallots, and cook, stirring frequently with a wooden spoon, until translucent and crisp-tender, 4 to 5 minutes. With a slotted spoon, transfer the shallots to a large serving bowl.

Add the remaining 2 tablespoons olive oil to the pan and when it is hot but not smoking add the red peppers. Cook over medium-low heat, stirring frequently with a wooden spoon, until just barely tender, about 10 minutes. Season the peppers with salt and pepper to taste and with a slotted spoon transfer them to the bowl with the shallots.

If using fresh corn, cut the kernels from the ears. Add the corn (fresh or frozen) to the skillet and cook, stirring frequently, until heated through, about 6 minutes for fresh, 3 minutes for frozen.

Add the garlic and crushed black peppercorns and stir to combine. With the slotted spoon, transfer the corn to the bowl with the shallots and peppers.

Add the thyme, parsley, white wine, and vinegar and stir to combine. Season with salt to taste and several grindings of pepper. Let the salad cool to room temperature, stirring occasionally.

SUMMER FRUIT SALAD WITH FRESH STRAWBERRY-YOGURT DRESSING

1 LARGE PINEAPPLE OR 4 CUPS CANNED
PINEAPPLE CHUNKS

1 CUP BLUEBERRIES

½ MEDIUM CANTALOUPE

1 PINT STRAWBERRIES

2 LIMES

1 CUP PLAIN LOWFAT YOGURT

2 TABLESPOONS HONEY

½ TEASPOON VANILLA EXTRACT

Halve the pineapple lengthwise, leaving the leaves on and cutting through the crown. Using a grapefruit knife (or other sharp flexible knife), loosen the fruit from the skin of the pineapple, leaving a ½-inch-thick shell; set the pineapple shells aside. Cut the cores out of the pineapple flesh and cut the fruit into bite-size pieces. Place the fruit in a medium bowl. Add the blueberries.

With a melon baller or teaspoon, scoop the flesh out of the cantaloupe half. Add the cantaloupe balls or pieces to the bowl.

Halve the strawberries and add half of them to the fruit in the bowl; set the remaining strawberries aside.

Grate the zest from the limes, then juice them. Add the lime juice and zest to the bowl of fruit and toss to combine.

Dividing evenly, scoop the fruit salad into the pineapple shells.

In a serving bowl, mash the remaining strawberries with a fork. Stir in the yogurt, honey, and vanilla and stir until combined.

Serve the pineapple halves on a platter, with the dressing on the side.

SUMMER FRUIT SALAD WITH FRESH STRAWBERRY-YOGURT DRESSING

TWO-BEAN SALAD WITH GRUYERE AND TOASTED PECANS

(PAGE 123)

BROCCOLI SALAD WITH RED ONION AND YELLOW PEPPER

(PAGE 101)

GREEK GREEN BEAN SALAD

1 POUND FRESH GREEN BEANS OR
2 PACKAGES (10 OUNCES EACH) FROZEN
WHOLE GREEN BEANS, THAWED

3 TABLESPOONS EXTRA-VIRGIN OLIVE OR
OTHER VEGETABLE OIL

3 TABLESPOONS RED WINE VINEGAR OR
CIDER VINEGAR

1 CLOVE GARLIC, MINCED OR CRUSHED
THROUGH A PRESS

2 TEASPOONS CHOPPED FRESH OREGANO
OR 1 TEASPOON DRIED

¼ TEASPOON FRESHLY GROUND
BLACK PEPPER

1 SMALL RED ONION, THINLY SLICED

½ CUP OIL-CURED PITTED BLACK OLIVES,
COARSELY CHOPPED

½ CUP CRUMBLED FETA CHEESE (ABOUT
2 OUNCES)

GREEK GREEN BEAN SALAD

Cut the green beans (fresh or frozen) into 2-inch lengths. (If using frozen green beans, simply drain them on paper towels.)

Place the fresh green beans in a vegetable steamer and bring the water to a boil. Steam the beans until crisp-tender, about 8 minutes. Cool the beans in a colander under cold running water.

Meanwhile, in a small bowl, combine the oil, vinegar, garlic, oregano, and pepper.

In a salad bowl, combine the steamed fresh green beans (or frozen, thawed), onion, olives, and dressing, and toss to coat well. Top the salad with the crumbled feta.

Serve the salad at room temperature or cover and chill until ready to serve.

HONEY-MUSTARD COLESLAW

½ POUND GREEN CABBAGE, TOUGH
OUTER LEAVES REMOVED

½ POUND RED CABBAGE, CORED AND
TOUGH OUTER LEAVES REMOVED

1 SMALL ZUCCHINI

1 SMALL CARROT

1 SHALLOT, MINCED

12 SMALL SWEET GHERKINS, EACH
SLICED ¼ TO ½ INCH THICK

JUICE OF 1 LEMON

1 TABLESPOON WHITE WINE VINEGAR

1 TABLESPOON CHOPPED FRESH DILL

1 TABLESPOON CHOPPED PARSLEY

¼ CUP PREPARED HONEY MUSTARD (OR
EQUAL PARTS DIJON MUSTARD
AND HONEY)

⅓ CUP MAYONNAISE

SALT AND FRESHLY GROUND
BLACK PEPPER

In a food processor or on the large holes of a box grater, finely shred the cabbages. Transfer the cabbage to a large mixing bowl and toss to combine the colors.

In the food processor or on the large holes of the grater, shred the zucchini and carrot. Add to the cabbage, with the shallot, gherkins, lemon juice, vinegar, dill, and parsley and toss to combine.

In a bowl, blend the honey mustard and mayonnaise. Spoon the mustard-mayonnaise over the slaw and toss until blended. Add salt and pepper to taste and toss again. Cover and chill thoroughly before serving.

TOMATO, ONION, AND ARUGULA SALAD

1 TEASPOON SESAME SEEDS

1 MEDIUM NAVEL ORANGE

1 POUND TOMATOES (3 OR 4 MEDIUM TO LARGE)

1 SMALL RED ONION

2 BUNCHES ARUGULA OR WATERCRESS, STEMMED

2 TABLESPOONS RED WINE VINEGAR

1 TEASPOON TAMARI OR ½ TEASPOON SOY SAUCE

JUICE OF ½ MEDIUM LEMON

SALT AND FRESHLY GROUND BLACK PEPPER

¼ CUP VEGETABLE OIL

In a small heavy skillet, toast the sesame seeds over medium heat until they turn golden brown and release their fragrance, 3 to 4 minutes.

With a paring knife, trim the peel and white pith from the orange. Separate the orange into sections. Coarsely chop the tomatoes into 1-inch chunks. Cut the onion into ⅛-inch slices.

In a salad bowl, combine the arugula, tomatoes, onion, and orange segments, and toss to combine.

In a small bowl, combine the vinegar, tamari or soy sauce, lemon juice, and salt and pepper to taste and whisk in the oil until the dressing is combined.

Pour the dressing over the salad, toss gently, and sprinkle the sesame seeds over the top.

FRESH CORN, LEEKS, AND PASTA SALAD WITH BASIL DRESSING

3 OUNCES PASTA SPIRALS

4 EARS FRESH CORN OR 1½ PACKAGES (10 OUNCES EACH) FROZEN KERNELS

2 CUPS WHITE PARTS OF LEEK, CUT INTO THIN ROUNDS

1 TABLESPOON FRESH LEMON JUICE

1 TEASPOON DIJON MUSTARD

⅓ CUP PLAIN LOWFAT YOGURT

¼ TEASPOON SALT

FRESHLY GROUND BLACK PEPPER

¼ CUP CHOPPED FRESH BASIL

2 LARGE TOMATOES, SLICED INTO THIN WEDGES

BLACK OLIVES, PITTED AND CHOPPED, FOR GARNISH

In a saucepan, bring 1 quart salted water to a boil over high heat. Add the pasta and cooking, stirring occasionally, until al dente, 6 minutes, or according to package directions. Drain the spirals in a colander, refresh under cold running water, and drain thoroughly. Transfer to a large bowl.

If using fresh corn, cook the ears in a large saucepan of boiling water for 6 to 10 minutes, until just tender. Refresh the ears under cold running water and drain them well. Using a sharp knife, cut the kernels from the cobs. If using frozen corn, blanch it in boiling water and drain it thoroughly. Add the corn to the pasta in the bowl.

In a saucepan of boiling water, blanch the leeks until just tender but still crisp, 1 to 2 minutes. Drain in a colander, refresh under cold running water, and drain well. Add the leeks to the bowl.

In a bowl, blend the lemon juice and mustard with the yogurt. Stir in the salt, some pepper, and the basil. Pour the dressing over the salad and toss gently to combine.

Transfer the salad to a platter and arrange the tomato wedges around the side; scatter the olive slices decoratively over the top.

TROPICAL FRUIT SALAD
WITH CANDIED GINGER

4 VERY RIPE PASSION FRUITS

½ HONEYDEW MELON, SCOOPED INTO
BALLS WITH A MELON BALLER

½ CANTALOUPE, SCOOPED INTO BALLS
WITH A MELON BALLER

½ PINEAPPLE, CORED AND CUT
INTO CHUNKS

2 GUAVAS, HALVED LENGTHWISE,
SEEDED, EACH HALF SLICED CROSSWISE

1 PINK GRAPEFRUIT, PEELED AND CUT
INTO SEGMENTS

2 PAPAYAS, PEELED AND SEEDED, FLESH
CUT INTO CHUNKS

1 LARGE MANGO, PEELED, FLESH CUT
LENGTHWISE INTO SLICES

¼ CUP CANDIED GINGER,
COARSELY CHOPPED

CHOPPED PECANS, FOR GARNISH
(OPTIONAL)

Cut the passion fruits in half crosswise. Using a teaspoon, scoop out the seeds and pulp from each fruit into a fine sieve set over a bowl. With the back of the spoon, press all the juice into the bowl; discard the seeds and fibrous pulp remaining in the sieve.

Place all the prepared fruits in a large serving bowl and pour on the passion fruit juice. Gently mix and turn the fruits in the bowl to coat with juice. Chill the fruit salad, covered with plastic wrap, in the refrigerator.

Just before serving, add the candied ginger and stir it gently but thoroughly into the fruit salad. Garnish with the chopped pecans, if desired, and serve the salad at once on slightly chilled plates.

ORANGE AND RADISH SALAD WITH CORIANDER SEED DRESSING

8 MEDIUM NAVEL ORANGES

1 LARGE RED ONION, THINLY SLICED CROSSWISE AND SEPARATED INTO RINGS

1 SMALL BUNCH RADISHES (6 TO 8), TRIMMED

⅓ CUP RED WINE VINEGAR OR TARRAGON VINEGAR

1 TEASPOON SZECHWAN PEPPERCORNS OR BLACK PEPPERCORNS

1 TABLESPOON CORIANDER SEEDS

SALT AND FRESHLY GROUND BLACK PEPPER

½ CUP EXTRA-VIRGIN OLIVE OIL

With a paring knife, trim the peel and remove the white pith from each orange. Holding each orange over a bowl, with a sharp knife, free the segments by cutting toward the center on each side of the membranes, letting the segments fall into the bowl. Add the onion slices to the bowl and combine.

Coarsely grate the radishes into the bowl. Using a wooden spoon, toss gently.

In small bowl, combine the vinegar, peppercorns, coriander seeds, and salt and pepper to taste and whisk in the oil until the dressing is combined.

Pour the dressing over the salad and toss gently until thoroughly coated.

SERVES 4

2 OR 3 SLICES LIGHT RYE OR OTHER
WHOLE-GRAIN BREAD, CRUSTS REMOVED,
CUT INTO ½-INCH CUBES

2 LARGE FIRM-RIPE PEARS

2 OUNCES EDAM OR GOUDA CHEESE,
CUT INTO MATCHSTICKS

¼ POUND FENNEL BULBS (ABOUT
2 SMALL), THINLY SLICED

1½ CUPS LOOSELY PACKED WATERCRESS,
STEMMED AND DIVIDED INTO SPRIGS

¼ THIN-SKINNED LEMON,
COARSELY CHOPPED

1 TEASPOON GRAINY MUSTARD

1 TABLESPOON HONEY

¼ CUP EXTRA-VIRGIN OLIVE OIL

SALT AND FRESHLY GROUND
BLACK PEPPER

PEAR, FENNEL, AND WATERCRESS SALAD WITH TART LEMON DRESSING

Preheat the oven to 350 degrees. Arrange the bread cubes on a baking sheet and toast them in the oven, turning them several times, until golden brown and crisp, about 20 minutes. Let cool.

Core the pears and dice them. Place them in a bowl of cold water with some lemon juice in it to prevent the pears from discoloring. With a slotted spoon, remove the pears to a salad bowl and add the cheese, and fennel, cooled croutons, and watercress sprigs.

In a ceramic bowl, combine the chopped lemon, mustard, and honey and whisk in the olive oil until combined well. Season with salt to taste and several generous grindings of pepper.

Pour the dressing over the salad and toss it gently until completely dressed.

½ POUND GREEN BEANS, CUT INTO
2-INCH LENGTHS

¼ CUP TARRAGON VINEGAR

1 TEASPOON DIJON MUSTARD

1 TEASPOON CHOPPED FRESH TARRAGON
OR ½ TEASPOON DRIED

½ TEASPOON SALT

¼ TEASPOON FRESHLY GROUND
BLACK PEPPER

1 TABLESPOON CAPERS (OPTIONAL)

2 MEDIUM SHALLOTS, MINCED, OR
2 TABLESPOONS MINCED ONION

1 CUP CHOPPED SCALLIONS (ABOUT
5 MEDIUM)

½ CUP OLIVE OIL

1 HEAD OF BIBB LETTUCE, TORN INTO
BITE-SIZE PIECES

SHAKER GREEN BEAN SALAD

In a large saucepan of simmering salted water, cook the beans until crisp-tender, 2 to 3 minutes. Drain, rinse under cold running water, and drain again. Cover the beans and refrigerate until ready to serve.

Just before serving, in a salad bowl, combine the vinegar, mustard, tarragon, salt, pepper, capers, if using, shallots, and scallions. Gradually whisk in the olive oil.

Add the green beans and lettuce, toss the salad gently, and serve.

SERVES 8

1 WATERMELON (ABOUT 6½ POUNDS)

6 FRESH FIGS, CUT LENGTHWISE
INTO EIGHTHS

½ POUND SEEDLESS RED GRAPES

JUICE AND GRATED ZEST OF 2 LARGE
ORANGES

GRATED ZEST OF 1 LEMON

1 TABLESPOON GINGER SYRUP, FROM A
JAR OF PRESERVED STEM GINGER

2 TABLESPOONS HONEY

CHOPPED FRESH MINT LEAVES,
FOR GARNISH

GINGERED FRESH FRUIT IN A WATERMELON BOAT

Slice off the top of the watermelon about one-fifth of the way down. With a large spoon, scoop out the flesh on the lid; remove the seeds, and cut the flesh into 1-inch chunks. Reserve the lid, covered with plastic wrap, in the refrigerator.

Run a long-bladed knife around the edge of the large piece of melon between the flesh and the skin, cutting down deeply and keeping as close as possible to the skin. Make a series of deep, parallel cuts, 1 inch apart, across the flesh, followed by a series of similar cuts at right angles to the first. Gently scoop out the long, square sections of flesh. Remove the seeds and chop the flesh into cubes. Use the large spoon to scrape the remaining flesh from the walls of the watermelon shell; seed it and cut it into pieces in the same manner. Reserve the watermelon shell, the cut section covered with plastic wrap, in the refrigerator.

Put all the cut watermelon into a large, heatproof bowl, and add the figs and grapes.

In a small, nonreactive saucepan, mix together the orange juice and zest, the lemon zest, the ginger syrup, and the honey. Bring the liquid slowly to a boil and pour it over the fruit. Stir to combine, and let the fruit cool for 5 minutes. Stir again, cover the bowl, and place it in the refrigerator for 1 hour. Stir the fruit occasionally as it chills.

To serve, transfer the fruit, including any syrup in the bowl, to the watermelon shell, garnish the fruit with the chopped mint, and place the lid, partially covering the fruit, on top.

2 CUCUMBERS (ABOUT 1½ POUNDS
TOTAL)

1 TABLESPOON WHITE WINE VINEGAR

2 TABLESPOONS FRESH LEMON JUICE

½ TEASPOON MINCED GARLIC

1 TABLESPOON CHOPPED FRESH DILL OR
1 TEASPOON DRIED

1 TABLESPOON CHOPPED FRESH MINT OR
1 TEASPOON DRIED

SALT

MINTED CUCUMBER SALAD

Peel the cucumbers and halve them lengthwise. With a small spoon, seed each half and discard the seeds. Cut the cucumbers into ⅛-inch dice.

In a bowl, combine the cucumbers with the vinegar and lemon juice, and toss until evenly coated. Add the garlic, dill, and mint and toss to combine.

Add salt to taste and toss. Cover the salad and chill until ready to serve.

TWO-BEAN SALAD WITH GRUYERE AND TOASTED PECANS

1 PACKAGE (9 OUNCES) FROZEN
GREEN BEANS, THAWED

½ POUND GRUYERE, EMMENTHALER,
JARLSBERG OR SWISS CHEESE

½ POUND MUSHROOMS

1 CAN (15¼ OUNCES) RED KIDNEY BEANS

1 CUP PECAN HALVES

⅓ CUP OLIVE OR OTHER VEGETABLE OIL

¼ CUP RED WINE VINEGAR OR
CIDER VINEGAR

2 TABLESPOONS GRAINY OR REGULAR
DIJON MUSTARD

1 CLOVE GARLIC, MINCED

2 TABLESPOONS CHOPPED PARSLEY
(OPTIONAL)

1 TEASPOON DRIED TARRAGON

¼ TEASPOON DRY MUSTARD

½ TEASPOON SALT

¼ TEASPOON FRESHLY GROUND
BLACK PEPPER

Drain the thawed green beans on several layers of paper towels to absorb excess moisture.

Grate the cheese. Thinly slice the mushrooms. Drain the kidney beans, rinse under cold running water and drain well.

In an ungreased skillet or toaster oven, toast the pecan halves. Set aside to cool.

In a salad bowl, beat together the olive oil, vinegar, Dijon mustard, garlic, parsley (if using), tarragon, dry mustard, salt, and pepper.

Add the mushrooms and toss to coat thoroughly.

Add the drained green beans and kidney beans and the grated cheese, and toss to combine.

Just before serving, add the toasted pecans and toss to distribute.

G-H-K

L-M